# DYADIC DEVELOPMENTAL PSYCHOTHERAPY

The standards of Dyadic Developmental Psychotherapy encompass the following:

First, the upkeep of a contingent, collaborative, sensitive, reflective, and emotionally empathic courting among the therapist and consumer is a number one precept of remedy. The therapist is chargeable for developing and keeping effective concordant intersubjective reviews (Stern, 1985; Trevarthen 2001) with the consumer and for supporting caregivers create those reviews with their children. Intersubjectivity is a complete emotional, reflective, and behavioral revel in of the different. It includes shared emotions (attunement), shared attention, and shared, complimentary intentions. It is the invention inside the courting of the different. Creating and keeping an alliance is the essential first segment of remedy. The creation

and upkeep of an alliance facilitates create a stable base, taking into account exploration, that's important for integration and, ultimately, recuperation.

Second, the caregivers' and therapist's states of thoughts with appreciate to attachment must be prepared and in large part resolved earlier than starting remedy with the kid. The therapist's and the caregiver's states of thoughts with appreciate to attachment has been determined to be very essential for remedy success (Tyrell et. al., 1999; Dozier, et al. 2001).

Third, PACE and PLACE describe the simple stance of the therapist and caregiver. PACE describes the therapist's obligation for developing a recuperation tempo of remedy via way of means of being playful, accepting, curious, and empathic. PACE permits the therapist to generate and adjust the rising emotional reviews which might be explored in remedy. PLACE refers back to the caregiver's obligation for developing a recuperation location or surroundings via way of means of being playful, loving, accepting, curious, and empathic. The number one distinction among PACE and PLACE is the dedication that caregivers have towards their infant as compared with the therapist; the Love aspect of PLACE.

Fourth, interactive restore is every other essential precept of remedy. Inevitable conflicts, misunderstanding, and errors that arise in all relationships are immediately addressed and repaired. This procedure helps emotional regulation. It is the obligation of the grownup to provoke and version this procedure.

Fifth, resistance is handled with PACE. Resistance is regarded as reflecting worry, shame, and the kid's beyond terrible reviews with caregivers. Resistance isn't a pejorative and must now no longer be interpreted as terrible. Resistance is regarded as an expression of worry and can mirror that the therapist has long past too a ways or too speedy for the consumer. Resistance can be regarded as an adaptive approach for handling scary and traumatic affect. The reaction to resistance will then be interactive restore or extra observe and much less lead of the observe-lead-observe aspect, that's defined below.

Sixth, the therapist constantly assesses (Becker-Weidman, 2010a) the caregiver's readiness to be a sensitive, responsive, insightful, reflective, and dedicated attachment discern for the kid. If the therapist has issues approximately the kid's emotional and mental protection, the therapist will hold to paintings with the caregiver with out the kid to assist the caregiver remedy some thing limitations exist for the caregiver's developing this stable base and experience of protection for the kid.

Parents and different caregivers are crucial to Dyadic Developmental Psychotherapy. Caregivers are the keystone for a way remedy proceeds and its final results. In many respects, the high-quality predictor of final results isn't "how disturbed" the kid is; as an alternative it's far the caregivers

(Becker-Weidman, 2010, Becker-Weidman, 2010a):

* State of thoughts with appreciate to attachment
* Reflective feature and reflective abilities
* Commitment
* Insightfulness
* Sensitivity

## Evidence-Based, Empirically Validated, Effective Treatment

Dyadic Developmental Psychotherapy is a fusion of numerous proof-primarily based totally and empirically confirmed concepts and strategies (Becker-Weidman, 2010; Becker-Weidman, 2011; Becker-Weidman and Hughes, 2008). Dyadic Developmental Psychotherapy is an powerful, proof-primarily based totally (Craven and Lee, 2006) and empirically confirmed remedy. Craven and Lee (2006) decided that Dyadic Developmental Psychotherapy is a supported and applicable remedy (class three in a six stage system). However, their evaluate changed into most effective primarily based totally on consequences from a partial initial presentation of ongoing follow-up research, finally finished and posted in 2006 (Becker-Weidman, 2006a; Becker-Weidman, 2006b). The first take a look at (Becker-Weidman, 2006a) in comparison the consequences of Dyadic Developmental Psychotherapy with different styles of remedy, "traditional care", 365 days after remedy ended. A 2nd take a look at (Becker-Weidman, 2006b) prolonged those consequences to 4 years after remedy ended. Based at the Craven and Lee classifications (Saunders et al. 2004), inclusion of these research might have led to Dyadic Developmental Psychotherapy being categorized as an proof-primarily based totally class 2, "Supported and in all likelihood efficacious". Since the improvement of Dyadic Developmental Psychotherapy, there had been empirical research demonstrating the effectiveness of Dyadic Developmental Psychotherapy posted with the aid of using this author (Becker-Weidman, 2006a, Becker- Weidman, 2006b). These research every had a pattern length of 64. The first take a look at (Becker-Weidman, 2006a) in comparison businesses of youngsters who met the standards for Reactive Attachment Disorder and Complex Trauma (Cook, et. al., 2003; Cook, et. al., 2005). The experimental institution acquired Dyadic Developmental Psychotherapy at The Center for Family Development, at the same time as the manage institution acquired different standardized remedies with the aid of using different certified experts at different clinics. The businesses have been matched and have been now no longer notably one-of-a-kind on a number of variables consisting of age, gender, duration of time in placement or adoption, and their pre-remedy rankings at the Child Behavior Checklist (CBCL) (Ackenbach, 1991) and diverse different demographic variables. Both businesses of youngsters had rankings withinside the scientific variety at the CBCL earlier than remedy. One 12 months after remedy ended, the children in the experimental group (Dyadic Developmental Psychotherapy treatment) had post-test scores on all scales of the CBCL that were in the normal range and that were statistically significantly different (lower) than their pre-test scores. The youngsters withinside the manage institution had post-take a look at rankings that remained withinside the scientific variety and have been now no longer statistically notably one-of-a-kind from their pre-take a look at rankings.

The 2nd take a look at (Becker-Weidman, 2006b) accompanied those equal households for 4 years after remedy ended. This take a look at observed that the youngsters who had acquired Dyadic Developmental Psychotherapy persevered to have CBCL rankings withinside the everyday variety, ultimate statistically notably decrease than their pre-take a look at CBCL rankings. Children withinside the experimental institution, who certainly persevered to obtain different remedy from different companies at different clinics, now no longer most effective had CBCL rankings that remained withinside the scientific variety, however on 4 of the CBCL scales their rankings have been statistically notably worse: Anxious/Depressed, Attention Problems, Rule-Breaking Behavior, and Aggressive Behavior.

The following tables summarize the consequences of the 2 empirical research stated above.

Dyadic Developmental Psychotherapy is an have an effect on-targeted own circle of relatives remedy primarily based totally on Attachment Theory (Bowlby 1980, 1988; Holmes, 1993) and attracts at the great of numerous formerly established, proof-primarily based totally approaches, strategies, and strategies which have a robust proof base. Dyadic Developmental Psychotherapy makes use of a number of concepts, interventions, and strategies with well-researched and empirically supported foundations. For example, Dyadic Developmental Psychotherapy is constant with the primary concepts of powerful remedy for complicated trauma (Cook et al., 2003, 2005). Cook, et. al., pick out six middle additives of complicated trauma interventions: 'safety, self-regulation, self-reflective statistics processing, stressful revel in integration, relational engagement, and effective have an effect on enhancement' (Cook et al, 2005 p. 395). Dyadic Developmental Psychotherapy emphasizes every of those six middle additives.

**Table 1. Statistical Analysis of Treatment Group Child Behavior Checklist Scores**

| | Pre-test | | Post-test | | | | 2nd post-test | | |
|---|---|---|---|---|---|---|---|---|---|
| **Measure** | **Mean** | **SD** | **Mean** | **SD** | **t-value** | **p-value** | **Mean** | **SD** | **t-test prob** |
| **Withdrawn** | **65** | **11.854** | | **6.04.897** | | **<.0001** | **56** | **6** | **.008** |
| **Anxious/depressed** | **62** | **10.558** | | **8.12.665** | | **.006** | **58** | **5** | **.006** |
| **Social Problems** | **67** | **9.7** | **59** | **5.54.376** | | **<.0001** | **56** | **5** | **.001** |
| **Thought problems** | **68** | **9.5** | **65** | **3.96.133** | | **<.0001** | **60** | **8** | **.02** |
| **Attention problems** | **72** | **12.557** | | **6.15.836** | | **<.0001** | **57** | **6** | **<.0002** |
| **Rule-breaking behavior** | **69** | **6.9** | **53** | **3.812.181** | | **<.0001** | **52** | **3** | **<.0001** |
| **Aggressive behavior** | **71** | **9.1** | **55** | **4.510.576** | | **<.0001** | **54** | **4** | **<.0001** |

**Table 2**
**Statistical Analysis of Control Group Child Behavior Checklist Scores**

**Pre- test**

Post- take a look at

2d post- take a look at

**Measure**

Mean SD Mean SD t-

**value**

p- value

Mean SDt-

**take a look at prob**

| | | | | | | | | |
|---|---|---|---|---|---|---|---|---|
| **Withdrawn** | **65** | **10.563** | **9.45** | **1.427** | **.16** | **71** | **49** | **.18** |
| **Anxious/depressed** | **62** | **10.660** | **10.3** | **1.060** | **.3** | **70** | **10** | **.03*** |

| | | | | | | | | |
|---|---|---|---|---|---|---|---|---|
| **Social Problems** | **64** | **11.165** | **11.25** | **-0.854** | **.4** | **65** | **2** | **.5** |

| | | | | | | | | | |
|---|---|---|---|---|---|---|---|---|---|
| **Thought problems** | **63** | **8.6** | **62** | **8.1** | **0.964** | **.33** | **67** | **8** | **.8** |
| **Attention problems** | **68** | **11.966** | | **10.8** | **0.927** | **.36** | **77** | **9** | **.02*** |
| **Rule-breaking behavior** | **67** | **7.4** | **66** | **9.6** | **1.8691** | **.07** | **81** | **4** | **.02*** |
| **Aggressive behavior** | **70** | **10.268** | | **9.4** | **0.919** | **.37** | **81** | **4** | **.02*** |

*** Statistically significant**

Other factors of Dyadic Developmental Psychotherapy which have been discovered to have a sturdy proof-base withinside the psychotherapy final results studies literature consist of the subsequent factors.

First, have an effect on arousal has been discovered to be vital for effective consequences in psychotherapy (Beutler et al., 2004). Affect arousal (executed through the Dyadic Developmental additives of follow-lead-follow, affective/reflective dialogue, and PACE, amongst different additives, is controlled withinside the context of the co-law of have an effect on and interactive repair) is a good sized subject matter in Dyadic Developmental Psychotherapy.

Second, explaining how the beyond can be persevering with to have an effect on gift behavior, emotions, and meanings has been discovered to be an powerful mode of remedy in 63% of research reported (Orlinsky et al., 1994).

Third, forming and preserving a healing alliance is a center precept of Dyadic Developmental Psychotherapy. The healing alliance has been proven to be crucial to a success remedy final results (Norcross 2001; Lambert and Ogles 2004). The use of PACE is anticipated to assist facilitate this. There is a good sized effective affiliation among final results and the healing bond (Lambert and Ogles, p. 308). In searching on the therapist's contribution to the healing alliance, a good sized effective affiliation with final results changed into additionally discovered. "The therapist's contribution changed into undoubtedly related to final results 67% of the time and by no means negatively implicated," (Lambert and Ogles, p. 321). "The most powerful proof linking manner to final results issues the healing bond or alliance," (Lambert and Ogles, p. 360).

Fourth, reputation is a good sized thing of Dyadic Developmental Psychotherapy and is a good sized detail withinside the "PACE" mindset. Affirmation (reputation, non-possessive warmth, or unconditional effective regard) changed into discovered to be a good sized thing in effective healing final results. Acceptance includes a wholly nonjudgmental stance directed in the direction of the thoughts, feelings, and intentions that symbolize the child's internal life.

Described differently, the introduction of concordant intersubjective reports or the extent of empathic information and private rapport has a widespread records of getting been proven to be vital elements in effective final results. There is now, "wellknown reputation of empathy as a thing in final results, which has been certainly showed once more in a cutting-edge meta-analysis," (Orlinsky et al. 2004, p. 350).

Fifth, Dyadic Developmental Psychotherapy has each cognitive and experiential dimensions. Both those dimensions have a big frame of empirical support. "The present studies is now extra than enough to warrant a probable valuation of experiential remedy in 4 vital areas: depression, tension disorders, trauma, and marital problems," (Elliott et al. 2004, p. 527).

Sixth, dating elements are vital for a success remedy final results (Lambert and Ogles 2004). The improvement of a steady base from which exploration can arise calls for the improvement and preservation of an alliance. It is those not unusualplace elements throughout cures that account for a good sized part of remedy final results. "A healing dating this is characterised through trust, warmth, information, reputation, kindness, and human wisdom," (Lambert and Ogles 2004, p. 180), is defined as a wide set of things which might be not unusualplace throughout cures and related to customer improvement. These very identical elements shape the center mindset of Dyadic Developmental Psychotherapy: PACE.

Overall such elements as empathy, the potential for reflection, intersubjective sharing of experience, the healing alliance, furthering reflection, deepening emotional processing, improving adaptive skills, growing and preserving the healing bond, therapist affirmation, verbal exchange attunement, and the bond of relatedness among therapist and affected person are all vital elements in psychotherapy final results and are all vital additives of Dyadic Developmental Psychotherapy.

# ATTACHMENT-FACILITATING PARENTING: CENTRAL FOR TREATMENT SUCCESS

In this monograph I use the time period mother and father withinside the wide feel to intend caregivers: mother and father, family worrying for a child, and childcare people in residential remedy centers, for example. The principles, additives, and

strategies of Dyadic Developmental Psychotherapy are used withinside the identical way with the aid of using these types of number one caregivers. Whether the number one attachment determine is a beginning determine, adoptive-determine, foster-determine, relative, or residential remedy middle body of workers member, the number one attachment determine can use this method to facilitate restoration.

Parents are the keystone of desirable remedy outcomes. The right practise of caregivers to interact in remedy and create a restoration PLACE (an acronym defined underneath, status for Playful, Loving, Accepting, Curious, and Empathic) is a vital and crucial thing of the remedy process. This phase affords a quick evaluate of this vital and crucial thing. A a good deal greater particular account of parenting and determine education regular with Dyadic Developmental Psychotherapy may be discovered withinside the book, Attachment Parenting (Becker-Weidman and Shell, 2010) and in numerous different publications (Becker-Weidman, 2010; Becker-Weidman, 2011; Becker-Weidman, 2006c; Hughes, 2007; Hughes, 2009; Ring 2011).

Helping caregivers see underneath floor conduct and seize a glimpse of the underlying feelings and perceptions riding that conduct is step one in assisting mother and father alternate the lenes via which they view their baby. The determine's assumptions and understandings approximately the kid's reasons, intentions, and functions without delay decide how the determine perspectives the kid and the revel in, and this without delay influences how the determine feels approximately the kid and the revel in. For example, a baby is discovered in her room together along with her brother's juice container and different meals gadgets withinside the closet, at the back of a few bins. If the determine's knowledge of this case is that the kid "stole" the gadgets and is hiding and being sneaky, the determine will experience one manner closer to the kid, in all likelihood aggravated and frustrated. If this has been the umpteenth time the determine instructed the kid now no longer to thieve her brother's juice bins and conceal meals in her closet, and whenever the kid is of the same opinion with the determine now no longer to do that, the determine may also now be feeling pretty disenchanted with the kid. On the opposite hand, if the determine is familiar with the kid's conduct as being pushed with the aid of using a distinct set of reasons and intentions, the determine will experience pretty in a different way. For example, if the determine is going deeper and recollects that the kid has grown up in settings wherein there has been inconsistent care giving, a loss of any dependable supply of meals, and nobody to assist the kid, then the determine may also view the kid's conduct as reflecting that revel in and being pushed with the aid of using worry of going hungry and a notion that the most effective one she will be able to anticipate is herself. In this instance, the determine may also have a good deal greater empathy for the woman and respond accordingly. By assisting mother and father see underneath the floor and apprehend the forces riding behaviors, the therapist can assist mother and father experience in a different way after which act in a different way, greater therapeutically, closer to their baby.

"All conduct is adaptive" and "type attributions" are critical concepts for the therapist to talk to the caregivers. All conduct is adaptive refers back to the belief that one develops in reaction to people, conditions, relationships, and stories that form how someone feels and acts. Behaviors increase which can be adaptive to the state of affairs wherein the ones behaviors at the start formed. In many respects "symptoms" may be regarded as behaviors that have been adaptive and that developed in reaction to a particular set of circumstances, however those identical behaviors are now "symptoms" due to the fact they now arise in new conditions wherein the behaviors are not adaptive. The new conditions are inhibited from having an impact on those antique behaviors if the antique stories nevertheless evoke the pressure reaction gadget on a continual basis. In those times it's far the "survival mind" and now no longer the" getting to know mind" this is by and large active. The survival mind does now no longer characteristic to contain new information, stories, or feelings. This is important for caregivers to apprehend, in order to attention on growing a restoration PLACE at domestic with a deep feel of emotional, psychological, and bodily safety.

Recognizing that every one conduct is adaptive as a precept can assist dad and mom appearance under the floor whilst offered with hard behaviors via way of means of their infant. Rather than attempting to "manage" or prevent conduct, it's miles plenty extra powerful to find out what's the driving force or motivation for the conduct and deal with that underlying engine. This may be hard for dad and mom to do whilst they may be withinside the center of a few enjoy with their infant at domestic, on the mall, withinside the grocery store, or at church. By assisting dad and mom awareness in this precept, *all conduct is adaptive*, the dad and mom might be advocated to recollect wondering approximately, "What goes on here?" or "I surprise what's making my infant act this manner?" The responses to those questions can lead the discern deeper and into extra powerful stories which create protection for his or her infant.

An instance may also serve to demonstrate the preceding factor. Six-year-antique Tanya and her father, Jared, are on the grocery store. Jared has simply instructed Tanya that they might now no longer be getting CoCo puffs however might get every other cereal (Tanya is allergic to chocolate). A few moments later, "suddenly" as she begins offevolved flailing withinside the buying cart, Tanya begins offevolved to yell loudly, "NO! You can't make me!" Jared's first idea is to inform her, "Stop yelling. You can't have CoCo puffs, and that's it!" He's feeling uncovered and embarrassed via way of means of his daughter's tantrum. But then he wonders, "Is Some thing else going on?" At that second he notices the tall bald guy on foot down the aisle and remembers that Tanya's start father shaved his head and that there has been a variety of very violent home violence in Tanya's start domestic. So, Jared, wondering that Tanya can be scared, alternatives her up out of the buying cart, hugs her, and whispers into her ear, "You are safe, Honey. I'm here, and I'll hold you safe, OK, Honey-bun?" Tanya blinks like she is waking up and appears at him, stops squirming, and says, "OK, Daddy." Was Jared proper approximately what he assumed turned into inflicting Tanya's episode? Maybe and perhaps now no longer. What did manifest is that Jared took a second to recollect what is probably making his daughter so dissatisfied (fear?). He then answered in a chilled way. That is the critical element. Jared created a bubble of protection, comfort, and protection that calmed his daughter. He did for her what she turned into not able to do for herself, alter her dissatisfied. This increases every other crucial factor for discern education in the context of Dyadic Developmental Psychotherapy. Parents set the rhythm, tone, and emotional weather for the own circle of relatives and for the infant. Jared acted in a way that was responsive to Tanya and engaged her a manner that led to her responding to him and his emotional state rather than Jared amplifying Tanya's emotional upset by becoming emotionally upset.

The precept of type attributions is associated with the precept of all *conduct is adaptive and has meaning*. When in doubt, characteristic benign motivations or intentions to the client. Helping a discern have type attributions concerning their infant's intentions is much more likely to cause the advent of tremendous concordant intersubjective stories and the advent of protection and protection, that is maximum conducive to the functioning of the gaining knowledge of brain. This identical precept applies to the therapist's information and dating with the dad and mom. While the conduct might not be laudable, most customarily the deeper aim is extra tremendous.

The following instance illustrates this factor. Roger and Kathy followed Keli from Columbia whilst she turned into 4 years antique. During our first interview they defined how now, via way of means of age nine, "She remains stealing meals and hoarding it in her bedroom. Whatever she wants, she simply steals, at domestic, in school, at the store." They defined how whilst they'd trap her, she'd first "lie" approximately stealing, then have a tantrum, and lots later say she turned into sorry, however her conduct in no way changed. Roger and Kathy had gotten to the factor in which they felt their domestic as like a jail, with meals locked up and their having to go looking Keli's backpack each day earlier than and after school. In our first meeting, which turned into simply with Roger and Kathy, we mentioned Keli's background, what they imagined and knew it turned into like for her, and the way that would still, possibly, be affecting her. Afterwards, the subsequent talk occurred.

Roger: She turned into hungry all of the time withinside the foster domestic in Columbia. When we were given her, Keli turned into so skinny she turned into underweight. She placed on ten kilos proper when we were given her.

Kathy: So meals's usually been crucial to her. She concerns a lot approximately it. now?

Therapist: So how may that have an effect on how she reports existence R:

Maybe she nevertheless concerns approximately it? But we've were given lots

of meals in
our home.

K: But Roger, we've usually attempted to govern her get entry to to meals, and we get irritated whilst she steals it. Maybe she's simply scared.

T: OK, Kathy, if that's so, that your Keli is genuinely concerned or frightened of being hungry and starved, due to the fact that's what existence in Columbia became like, then perhaps she's simply attempting to attend to herself. Maybe she's simply looking to make sure she has meals whilst her expectation is that meals might not be round whilst she is hungry. And whilst she were given hungry in Columbia, she were given REALLY hungry, she became starving.

R: Oh, I sense so bad, have we harm her more?

K: (begins offevolved to cry) We have been all wrong. Oh our bad little Keli, what can we do now?

T: You sense badly which you didn't see this earlier than and remorse the way you dealt with Keli.

K: Yes, I do. Is it too late?

T: Roger, how do you
sense?

R: I sense horrible and (to Kathy) I suppose we will restoration it?

K: Do you?

R: Yes.

T: I can sense how an awful lot you need to assist Keli and the way regretful you are. You see what she is doing so in a different way now, thru her experience, that makes feel to you?

K: Well, first of all, I suppose we want to ensure she has meals round her and that we provide her what she can be desiring in order that she will be able to genuinely understand we are able to contend with her.

T: Maybe her aim wasn't to scouse borrow, perhaps her aim became to try and get what she thinks she wants and needs for herself due to the fact she hadn't skilled caregivers as worrying or giving.

R: That have to be it. (Laughing) Now, if I can simply preserve remembering that, I won't be so irritated once I discover a yogurt box in her room.

In this example, if the dad and mom count on that Keli's is a thief and intends to scouse borrow from others what isn't hers, the dad and mom will sense one manner and act accordingly. If we assist the dad and mom to have type attributions, and recognize that each one conduct is adaptive and has meaning, then the dad and mom can appearance underneath the floor to look how Keli's taking meals and hoarding may also don't have anything to do with stealing and feature the entirety to do with a deep fear, grounded in her existence experience, of starving. This will lead the dad and mom to sense pretty in a different way and act pretty in a different way. This distinction will assist create a more feel of protection and safety for Keli, who will then be much more likely to start to contain those new reports into her inner running fashions of caregivers.

There are numerous different crucial factors of attachment facilitating parenting which are grounded in Dyadic Developmental Psychotherapy that the therapist will need to talk to the dad and mom. Parents can honestly study those numerous factors via way of means of studying books or articles, and therapists can "train" dad and mom the usage of psycho-academic fashions. However, early in treatment, and that is whilst the fabric is imparted, it's miles beneficial to consider that the therapist's attention is on constructing and keeping a stable base. At instances simply telling the caregivers what to do and why may be effective. Often, even inside that first session, the dad and mom sense sufficient protection and luxury that direct education is preferred and effective. However, regularly there are instances

whilst the therapist will locate it healing to awaken the fabric and concepts via way of means of exploring with the dad and mom their thinking, their feeling states, their reports as dad and mom, and their know-how in their child. Using PACE and follow-lead-follow, the therapist can discover all of those regions and assist dad and mom come to a deeper know-how of themselves and in their child.

While telling mother and father what to do and the way to do it is able to appear like an expedient strategy to the problems of operating with wounded mother and father, it's miles now no longer. While coaching a person to "fish" takes a good deal longer than simply giving them the "fish," gaining knowledge of to fish will, withinside the lengthy run, boom their feel of efficacy, self-concept, and competency. Whatever the therapist wishes the caregiver so that you can do with the kid, the therapist has so that you can do with the determine. Modeling and developing the reviews with the determine that the therapist needs the determine to create with the kid is a good deal greater effective and lengthy-lasting than imparting a lecture on what to do. When caregivers find out their capacities and discover new approaches of referring to and being, the determine is more likely to "own" the revel in and for those new approaches of being (those modified inner operating models) to turn out to be incorporated into the person's autobiographical narrative.

It is vital that caregivers have fairly nicely advanced capacities concerning their sensitivity, insightfulness, kingdom of thoughts with recognize to attachment, commitment, and reflective characteristic earlier than going too a ways withinside the consultation with the kid. The caregivers do want so that you can create a few feel of protection and protection with the kid for the paintings to continue from growing and keeping an alliance to exploration. When operating with households wherein the caregivers have confined capacities in those regions, the therapist will want to assist caregivers broaden the capacities. The volume to which the therapist can have interaction in exploration of painful and hard regions with the kid and own circle of relatives is ruled through the caregivers' capacities concerning sensitivity, insightfulness, commitment, reflective characteristic, and kingdom of thoughts with recognize to attachment. When caregivers have obstacles in those regions and the therapist is operating to assist broaden the ones capacities, the paintings in own circle of relatives periods with the kid will step by step circulate greater deeply because the caregiver's capacities improve.

## Phases of Treatment

This segment in brief summarizes the levels of Dyadic Developmental Psychotherapy. The levels arise in a recursive and repetitive way, similar to the levels of the moon. The levels overlap and arise in a cyclical way and so must now no longer be taken into consideration discrete or rigidly described. The cost of thinking about those levels is that the diverse additives of Dyadic Developmental Psychotherapy are used in another way withinside the distinctive levels of remedy (Becker-Weidman, 2010; Becker-Weidman, 2011). Like a persistent spiral, improvement and remedy maintain ever deeper. As remedy proceeds, the therapist ought to always paintings to preserve the alliance, discover to gain integration and healing, after which make certain that the alliance stays robust sufficient to continue. Exploration and integration can cause a greater stable alliance, for you to permit for deeper exploration and in addition integration and healing. Healing frequently lets in a more potent alliance to broaden, for you to facilitate in addition integration. While the overall ideas continue to be constant, every segment calls for a distinctive blend of the additives of Dyadic Developmental Psychotherapy. It is the utility of the diverse additives of Dyadic Developmental Psychotherapy in a differential way this is the artwork of this remedy. One segment can also additionally remaining numerous periods, and lots of levels can be found in one consultation. Healing can also additionally start withinside the first actual consultation, for example. The levels defined right here are described in phrases of attachment theory: growing and keeping the alliance (stable base), exploration, integration, and healing. An alliance is vital to create and preserve a stable base. A stable base is vital to start exploration. Exploration ends in integration. Integration is the idea for healing.

# DEVELOPING THE ALLIANCE

Developing the alliance is a vital segment of remedy. Without an alliance, there may be no exploration, integration, and healing. Children and mother and father or carers with unresolved traumas and hurts may have a greater hard time forming an alliance with the therapist. In those instances, the therapist will ought to pay precise interest to growing the alliance and relationship.

Creating a stable base in remedy turns into one of the therapist's number one task. There are 4 number one duties on this segment:

* Forming a healing alliance.
* Developing a remedy contract. Why are we right here? Why are we meeting? What are we doing right here?
* Forming preliminary theories of behavior: the meanings to be explored.
* Creating a steady base.

While all additives of Dyadic Developmental Psychotherapy can be used, some stand out as extra salient on this phase: PACE, the "observe" measurement of observe-lead-observe, intersubjectivity, and the co-law of affect. Creating a steady base after which retaining that alliance is a necessary and essential precursor to beginning the Exploration phase. Therapist's use of self is likewise an essential thing in growing a steady base in treatment. The therapist need to be emotionally engaged withinside the intersubjective stories inside treatment, and this calls for exact self-awareness, reflective abilities, and insightfulness at the a part of the therapist. In operating with dad and mom and caregivers, it's also essential to assist them admire the significance of the construct, "It's approximately connections, now no longer compliance," (Becker-Weidman, 2010, Hughes and Becker-Weidman, 2010).

In this case I am that specialize in constructing an alliance with each father and daughter; each have a alternatively significant trauma history.

Barry (Dad): It's been a horrible week. Megan had a number of tantrums.

Note: While Dad is pronouncing this, Megan, age 11, is sitting there with a scowl on her face and fingers crossed.

Therapist: (to Dad and Megan) Oh, you each had a hard week, it sounds like. Not a laugh at all.

Megan: No, I had to mention in my room. B: Well, you …

T: (therapist interrupts right here) I wonder, Barry, what you could have performed for a laugh if you'd had a higher week?

Note: The therapist intervenes to alternate the tone of the interplay and pass farfar from a blaming/shaming interplay that each Dad and Megan are used to, and into an interplay that has a extra effective emotional tone so that it will construct a effective enjoy withinside the room with them and construct the alliance. Now, it's miles essential to emphasise that what I am now no longer pronouncing is that withinside the early periods the therapist tries to keep away from conflicts and

disagreements. The therapist does need to break blaming/shaming interactions and attempt to technique the struggle in a extra effective way. Alternatively, the therapist would possibly be aware the struggle after which come lower back to it later withinside the session. In any event, it's miles essential to now no longer keep away from conflicts and variations. It is the way wherein those variations and disagreements are dealt with this is essential.

B: Hey, if we may want to have long gone to the beach, that might were a laugh, proper Megan?

M: (nonetheless searching sullen, she factors to a photo and she or he mumbles) Is that a shark?

T: Yes, it's miles. (Follow a part of observe-lead-observe)

M: (displaying extra hobby and searching at me for the primary time) Weren't you scared?

T: No, the dive leaders made certain we stayed secure and informed us approximately what to do and now no longer do whilst we have been down there. (Turning to Barry): What do you believe you studied of that photo? (Moving into the lead a part of observe-lead- observe)

B: I'd like to take Megan snorkeling; I wager she'd like

it. T: Why don't you ask her?

B: (to Megan) Would you want to head snorkeling?

M: Not if there are sharks around. (Still use to a bad interplay together along with her dad, she acts in a way, now no longer consciously of course, to awaken a sample that feels familiar)

T: Dad, what made you believe you studied Megan would love snorkeling (Here I try to preserve the point of interest on some thing extra effective and start a father- daughter talk).

B: Oh, I understand she loves the water. She's been on a swim group on the Y for 2 years now and does great. I'm without a doubt proud of ways tough she works at it.

M: (now seems at Dad for the primary time) Maybe I'd like snorkeling.

Would you go together with me?

We see right here how the therapist makes use of a non-public hobby to interact each father and daughter. The therapist makes use of observe-lead-observe to deepen the

enjoy and pass it right into a dating centered interplay and a talk among father and daughter.

# MAINTAINING THE ALLIANCE

Maintaining the alliance is a segment that the therapist have to cope with all through remedy. At times, it's miles withinside the vanguard of the work, and at different times, it recedes into the background. Focusing in this segment turns into mainly critical while there was a few breach withinside the alliance or dating and interactive restore turns into a outstanding factor utilized by the therapist or figure. The therapist's use of self is also an critical factor on this segment. When the therapist or figure has made a mistake, it's miles crucial to remedy that neither permit disgrace to prevent acknowledging the error that has been made and the breach that consequences. One of the therapist's number one obligations is to preserve a recovery and healing tempo of remedy. As defined elsewhere (Becker-Weidman, 2010), it isn't always errors that reason troubles in remedy. It is the shortage of acknowledgement and restore of these errors that creates troubles in remedy.

Once the alliance has been formed, the therapist acts to deepen, beef up, and preserve the alliance. As with the opposite stages, this segment overlaps the opposite stages, and the opposite stages cycle returned to this segment. For example, Exploration that ends in Integration and Healing allows Maintain and beef up the alliance.

The number one obligations of Maintaining the Alliance are:

* Deepening and strengthening the healing alliance
* Managing emotional proximity
* Exploring preliminary theories of behavior: the meanings to be explored.
* Repairing dating breaches.

Five additives of Dyadic Developmental Psychotherapy are mainly salient in the course of this segment of remedy: PACE, intersubjectivity, comply with-lead-comply with, interactive restore, and the co-law of affect. In this 2d segment of remedy, the therapist will need to pay unique interest to the usage of comply with-lead-comply with as the start technique into the exploration segment. How the purchaser responds to the "lead" step of comply with-lead-comply with is a degree of ways quick and deeply the therapist can circulate into exploration

and a degree of the electricity and intensity of the alliance. This segment of remedy takes on much less significance as remedy progresses due to the fact later in remedy the purchaser has skilled the therapist's intentions as being useful and exploration, integration, and recovery have caused a greater bendy and reality-focused inner running model. Later in remedy, the therapist does now no longer ought to attention as lots on keeping the alliance due to the fact the alliance has more emotional intensity and electricity. The purchaser could have skilled the therapist's intentions to be useful, and the purchaser could have skilled the effective consequences of hard explorations.

In the subsequent vignette, the therapist is speaking with a foster mom early in remedy. They have a starting dating, Ms. Kay is understandably cautious. This is the fourth therapist she's been to withinside the 3 years she's had Barry, all with out a change, assist, or maybe appreciation for a way hard dwelling with Barry can be.

Therapist: Hi, Grace, how's the week been?

Ms. Grace Kay: Awful, you haven't any idea.

T: What passed off? (Accepting and being curious)

G: Barry changed into a stinker; he lied to me approximately now no longer doing his homework, and I took his I-Pod, after which he screamed at me so I despatched him to his room.

T: (instead of cope with the punitive great of the area in a lecture, at this early segment of keeping the alliance, the therapist actions to apply ACE and comply with-lead-comply with to bolster the alliance and stable base of remedy) That sounds awful, you have to were genuinely upset.

G: What's incorrect with him? He's been with me almost  years, and I need to undertake him and he is aware of it. Why could he lie approximately his homework? He is aware of how I sense approximately lying!

T: It genuinely is odd, isn't it? I imply you care approximately him and also you try and assist him with school. What could make him now no longer inform the reality approximately his homework? What's your guess?

G: He didn't need to get in problem with me!

T: Oh, what could have passed off if he'd advised you he'd now no longer performed his homework?

G: Nothing, I'd have requested him if he wanted assist, after which I'd assist him. He is aware of that!

T: That's strange. Since he'd now no longer were in problem if he'd advised you he didn't or couldn't do his homework, what could make him now no longer inform you?

G: I don't know. I can't discern that boy out.

T: Well, if he honestly believed you have been there to assist him, wouldn't he come to you?

G: I guess.

T: So, if we study his conduct as a message to us approximately how he feels and the way he sees relationships, what does his hiding his now no longer doing his homework inform us? (The therapist maintains to word statements in a joining, "you and me together" type of manner)

G: He need to now no longer accept as true with me, however why? It's been nearly  years?

T: Ok, that makes feel. Barry doesn't let you know due to the fact he doesn't accept as true with you. Maybe he's frightened of some thing horrific occurring to him, of your doing some thing horrific. Why might he suppose that?

G: Hmmm. His start own circle of relatives turned into honestly abusive. He got here to me with a damaged arm and 3 damaged ribs, and he's had as a minimum 3 cranium fractures. Maybe he thinks if he doesn't do what I need, like his homework, I'll harm him like they did.

T: That makes feel. So, what you're telling me is that perhaps he turned into afraid to inform you he couldn't do his domestic work. Then he needed to make up a tale to cowl that up due to the fact he turned into afraid he'd get harm?

G: Yes, that would be.

T: Ok, so if we observe your theory, and it honestly makes feel, Grace, then what will be the nice technique?

G: Oh my, sending him off and punishing him in all likelihood simplest made him sense worse.

Comment: So, Grace now has a brand new knowledge of her foster-son's conduct and this leads her to a brand new knowledge of the way to technique him. The therapist starts the use of recognition and observe-lead-observe to increase the alliance similarly in order that exploration of latest meanings of Barry's conduct can

begin.

# EXPLORATION

Exploration calls for a steady base (an alliance) and might arise withinside the first actual meeting. Exploration calls for a feel of safety (physical, emotional, and psychological) and security. There are 4 number one obligations for the duration of the Exploration segment. The aim is to discover history, memories, occasions, and reviews that retain to form the client's relationships and that retain to have an effect on conduct and functioning. Primary obligations on this segment are:

* Exploring how the beyond is alive withinside the present.
* Exploring of inner operating models.
* Exploring the meanings of occasions and conduct.
* Developing the reflective feature.

The number one additives of Dyadic Developmental Psychotherapy which might be specially essential on this segment are: PACE, developing and retaining intersubjectivity, growing the reflective feature, insightfulness, observe- lead-observe, interactive repair, commitment, co-introduction of that means, and the co-law of have an effect on. Of these, the co-introduction of that means and the co- law of have an effect on are in particular essential. PACE results in Concordant intersubjectivity. Concordant intersubjectivity, interactive repair, and the reflective feature assist co-adjust emotions. The affective/reflective communicate and insightfulness, together with PACE, facilitate the co-introduction of that means.

Joseph lived together along with his 3 start-brothers and his adoptive dad and mom. Joseph turned into the youngest. Joseph turned into eliminated from his start mom from the medical institution and positioned in foster take care of years earlier than getting into the Jones' domestic together along with his brothers. In the primary a part of this primary session, I'd met with the dad and mom by myself for approximately 1/2 of an hour. The following is from that session:

Margaret: He receives so argumentative while me or Mitch suggest anything.

Therapist: I marvel what might make him get so indignant and, as you've defined it, defiant? (I am looking to amplify their view and increase their insightfulness into Joe's conduct)

Mitch: Maybe he simply loves to argue

T: (accepting that). Ok, what might make him need to argue?

Mitch: I don't know, that's why we're here.

T: Well, the 2 of you could have a few guesses.

Margaret: I suppose he simply argues with us, however then later while he's had a risk to reflect onconsideration on it, he does come returned and could speak with us or even receive our ideas.

T: So, you're looking to assist him, looking to be helpful, and he's type of combating you.

Marg: Yes.

T: It's nearly like he need to understand what you're doing as a horrific aspect or a hurtful aspect. I suggest the manner he reacts doesn't appear like he sees what you're doing as looking to be helpful.

Marg: No, we're now no longer arguing with him or looking to get right into a fight. (Both Margaret and Mitch have a hard time seeing how Joseph can also additionally enjoy the arena so in a different way than they do).

T: You're looking to be helpful, right? Marg: Yes

T: So perhaps it's like "telephone." The message sent, which you need to assist him, isn't the message received. Maybe he hears some thing specific.

Mitch: I don't recognise. I've had numerous discussions with him that we don't like his arguing and his defiance and that we're seeking to assist him. He appears to get it, however then he begins offevolved throughout again.

T: It is confusing

Mitch: He simply doesn't get it.

T: Maybe his view of the connection or the speak is specific than yours. I say that due to the fact his response is so specific that what you every assume it need to be.

Marg: Yes, it is.

Comment: I don't appear if you want to hook up with the dad and mom and assist them see what I see, so I drop this subject matter and we communicate approximately how Joseph (Joe) is doing in college and some different things. This is an instance of

therapist use of self, the significance of the therapist's reflective capabilities, and of the therapist now no longer turning into too firmly wedded to 1 idea. By final bendy and keeping a non-stop kingdom of cognizance of the ebb and waft of feelings and procedure withinside the consultation and my effect on this, I am capable of act in a healing way and keep away from simply lecturing or arguing. I focus instead on developing and maintaining a secure base with the parents by focusing on PACE and giving them a lot of empathy about how hard they are trying and how difficult it's been these past thirteen years. Then I pass get Joe to enroll in us. About fifteen mins into the consultation with Joseph, age fifteen, we had the subsequent interchange.

Therapist: Hi, Joe, how are you?

Joe: fine.

T: (To Dad; Joe is sitting among Mom and Dad at the couch) Is he as tall as you? (I start via way of means of noticing some thing approximately the own circle of relatives to start our communicate)

Dad: (Joe sits up now) Taller, see?

Mom: He's manner taller than me.

Dad: Yep, he's tall and lanky (Joe has a at a loss for words appearance on his face). Joe: I'm now no longer lanky

Dad: Do you understand what lanky way? Joe: No.

Dad: It way tall and thin.

T: What made you are saying which you're now no longer lanky in case you didn't recognise what it way? (Curious approximately his reaction and what's below it)

J: You need to constantly say "No" to a query in college.

T: (Eyes wide, in a playful tone) Always? Like if a trainer asks you when you have a corridor pass, and also you do. You need to say no?

J: No, however to any query whilst you don't recognise the word, say "No."

Mom: Why?

J: Because on every occasion you get requested a query, it's horrific.
T: So your default role is "NO!" (I lead Joe a chunk deeper right here) J: Right, due to the fact it'll be horrific.

T: Oh, so, like while your mother or dad asks you some thing, it's gonna be horrific, so "No" is type of your default role? (Now I lead the dialogue deeper to discover how his inner operating version can also additionally have an effect on his enjoy of his dad and mom)

J: Yea.

T: (to dad and mom) So Joe's default role appears to be that questions suggest some thing horrific is withinside the works. That's type of what we have been speakme approximately in advance earlier than Joe got here in. (In this interchange I need to attach our preceding dialogue to what's taking place right here and now)

Dad: What do you suggest?

T: Oh, while we have been speakme earlier than Joe got here in approximately how your intentions whilst you ask Joe some thing are to be useful however that commonly an issue develops, so it appeared such as you suggest to be useful however perhaps Joe perceives your intentions differently: his default is that some thing horrific goes to happen.

D: Oh, yea, right.

T: (to Joe) Do you understand what we're announcing? J: No.

T: Maybe your dad and mom ought to provide an explanation for it. Who do you need to ask? J: I don't care.

T: OK, so who will you ask?

J: Ummm, both (then turns to Dad). Can you provide an explanation for it?

D: What we're announcing Joe is that once we ask approximately your day or ask you to do some thing, we suggest to assist you.

J: Whenever we take a seat down on the desk for a dialogue, you're criticizing me. I recognise if we take a seat down on the desk, I'm in trouble.

D: We need to assist you, and also you don't see that. You assume which you are in trouble.

J: Oh, now I get it.

T: So come what may your dad and mom have suitable intentions, and also you don't see it that manner.

J: No, I don't.

T: Wow, that should be so difficult for you, Joe, to regularly assume your

dad and mom don't have suitable intentions towards you. No surprise you and your dad and mom argue so much. They assume they may be seeking to be useful and also you don't experience they may be after which say "NO!" after which they push on, and also you get extra annoyed, and that they get extra annoyed.

J: It's now no longer fun.

T: So, might that be some thing you'd all like, to be a happier own circle of relatives and now no longer argue as much?

Mom, Dad, Joe: (At the identical time) Yes!

At the cease of this consultation I meet in brief with the dad and mom to talk about the consultation and the subsequent interchange occurred:

Therapist: So, what did you watched of the consultation? Dad: I'll ought to alternate how I communicate to Joseph.

T: What do you imply?

D: If he's now no longer getting what I imply I'll simply ought to attempt to get it across

better.

T: Oh, you imply like if perhaps you have been greater specific approximately what is

your intention. Saying some thing like, "Joe, I actually have an concept right here that I assume can be helpful, can I inform you?" Or, "Joe, I need to invite you some thing so we are able to parent this out collectively."

D: (laughing) That's good, yes. Can you write that down for me? (We all snigger at that).

Initially the dad and mom did now no longer appear to apprehend what I become trying to explain, a brand new that means for Joe's behavior. It may also were that due to the fact this become our first consultation collectively we simply did now no longer have sufficient of a stable base in location for that form of exploration to arise in order that my try become premature. In the consultation, even as retaining concordant intersubjectivity amongst all own circle of relatives participants and the usage of a comply with-lead-comply with layout in the PACE framework, the own circle of relatives experienced, in preference to intellectually heard, Joe's misperception. The affective/reflective talk that ensued enabled the own circle of relatives to enjoy the interaction, mirror at the interaction, after which increase a brand new that means. The new that means become that Joe become now no longer arguing to argue or to be defiant, he become seeking to shield himself and seeking to keep away from being in trouble.

Interchanges inclusive of the ones above that rely upon reminiscence of beyond stories are one manner to have interaction in exploration.

# INTEGRATION

Integration takes place in a cyclic manner. Exploration results in Integration, which permits for deeper exploration and in addition Integration and Healing. Integration consists of neurological integration, emotional integration, and mental integration. Its hallmark is the ability to peer sun sunglasses of grey in place of absolutes. Integration is visible whilst a purchaser is capable of maintain disparate feelings on the identical time. Integration takes place time and again in remedy and over time. In many regards, it's far a developmental system wherein stories, memories, events, relationships, emotions, and one's autobiographical narrative are transformed in a bendy manner. Many intellectual fitness problems may be considered as representing a loss of integration. For example, the flashbacks related to Post Traumatic Stress Disorder and Complex Trauma are a feature of the dearth of integration of episodic and implicit memories. Many of the cognitive problems related to Complex Trauma are a feature of intricate neurological integration.

Integration calls for that beyond events, situations, and stories be reviewed and revisited (exploration) in order that the inner operating fashions may be made specific, situation to exploration, and new meanings thereby created. The new meanings constitute a brand new integration of feelings and cognitions. It is maximum beneficial to think about integration as a system or spiral. In this view, developmental obligations run vertically, and integration is an ascending spiral that returns to every detail in a deeper and deeper fashion. In this manner, the character achieves extra ranges of integration over time (Becker-Weidman, 2010).

The number one challenge of Integration is the developmental of a coherent autobiographical narrative. Creating a coherent autobiographical narrative entails elements: one, the mixing of trauma and discount of splitting off implicit from episodic memories, and second, an more suitable reflective feature. Within this section the Dyadic Developmental

Psychotherapy additives which might be maximum applicable are: PACE, the affective/reflective talk, and co-introduction of that means. During this section, which may also represent the majority of remedy towards the center and cease of remedy, a overview of the purchaser's existence tale and a mirrored image at the purchaser's

contemporary country and the way the beyond may also nevertheless be energetic withinside the gift make up a massive percentage of remedy. Exploration and Integration arise in tandem and beef up every other. Exploration results in Integration, and Integration permits for deeper Exploration.

The following instance illustrates integration in treatment. Peter had an extended records of being abused and unnoticed with the aid of using his delivery dad and mom. He became eliminated from his delivery own circle of relatives on the age of six due to more than one cranium and arm fractures. Peter became in 5 foster homes, in the course of the subsequent 3 years. He became eliminated from one due to overlook and that foster domestic became closed. At age 9 he moved into the Therapeutic Foster domestic of Mr. and Mrs. Hunter and their 3 teenage sons. When Peter first moved into the Hunter domestic, he became nevertheless soiling himself, could hoard meals in his bed, regularly took gadgets now no longer his with out permission, and could emerge as competitive and violent towards Mrs. Hunter. Now 11 years antique and after ten months of treatment, Mr. and Mrs. Hunter and Peter are reflecting on their latest interchange approximately Peter's problems in faculty with bullies.

Mrs. Hunter: Peter got here to me weeks in the past due to the fact older women had been scary him, pronouncing suggest matters to him approximately him and us.

Therapist: Really? Peter, what became occurring?

Peter: These women had been being without a doubt suggest. They'd say I became dumb and smelled horrific. They'd say my mother became fats and all varieties of matters that made me without a doubt mad.

Therapist: So what happened?

Peter: Well before everything I simply attempted to deal with it myself, and I didn't accomplish that well. I'd get indignant and begin yelling, and I even driven Eloise once, er twice, actually.

Therapist: So you then definately went on

your dad and mom? Peter: Yes

Mr. Hunter: It became without a doubt good. We'd recognized some thing became occurring due to the fact he'd gotten some demerits in faculty for yelling at those women withinside the corridor and pushing one.

Therapist: So, Peter, what made you visit your dad and mom?

Peter: I found out what I became doing wasn't working. I additionally found out

a part of what made me so indignant with the ones women is that a number of what they stated and did jogged my memory of the way my sisters could bully me and the way my birthparents concept that became humorous and could egg them on. I found out that I need to inform Mom and Dad due to the fact they're now no longer like my delivery dad and mom

Mrs. Hunter: When he advised us what became occurring, we found out that the faculty became simplest listening to one aspect of this. They'd see Peter yelling or pushing, however he didn't inform them what the women had completed to initiate him. After he advised us, I known as the predominant and advised her what became occurring.

Peter: Yea, she did, and I felt so good. Mom became supporting me! (He says this in a glad loud voice with a massive smile)

Therapist: You appearance so glad now approximately that.

Peter: You guess I am. Getting in hassle was what I became, however now no longer now. Now, every now and then horrific matters happen, however I've were given human beings to assist me (searching from Mom to Dad with a massive smile).

Mr. Hunter: What made me sense without a doubt happy with Peter became that he's been going to the steerage counselor each day to inform him what those women are doing and pronouncing. And wager what? Peter hasn't had any demerits in weeks, and one of the women became simply suspended on the quit of this week.

Therapist: Way to head Peter!

In this short interchange we will see how the affective/reflective speak lets in Peter and his dad and mom to co-create a brand new which means for Peter. The new which means is that Peter can ask for assist and gets it. This new which means results in a widespread alternate in his self-concept, his feeling state, and his behavior.

## HEALING

Healing happens all through treatment. Healing isn't a lot a separate section as it's far, in part, an outgrowth of Integration. Integration is a recuperation process. However, it's far vital to be aware that the improvement and protection of an alliance may be recuperation in and of itself. The improvement of an emotionally significant dating is recuperation and might treatment a number of the results of early, continual maltreatment that has happened inside a care- giving dating. The consequences of recuperation consist of the improvement of a

extra complex, nuanced, and included autobiographical narrative and a better-evolved reflective function. A few of the additives of Dyadic Developmental Psychotherapy that can be extra salient in the course of Healing consist of the following: co-advent of recent meanings, insightfulness and reflection, affective/reflective speak, and PACE.

As remedy is ending, there's accelerated time spent reflecting at the remedy reviews and a party of ways lifestyles is different. This isn't to mention that the therapist does now no longer observe and touch upon high-quality reviews in every consultation. Often an crucial detail of every consultation is the mirrored image on what right has occurred. This mirrored image on high-quality modifications and a party of the lengthy and hard adventure is an crucial detail of starting to stop remedy and integration of the revel in. This technique enables body the remedy revel in and locate its location withinside the own circle of relatives narrative. During this technique, all of the additives of Dyadic Developmental Psychotherapy may be evident.

# COMPONENTS OF DYADIC DEVELOPMENTAL PSYCHOTHERAPY

These additives include:

1. Therapist use of self
2. Process focused: It's approximately connections now no longer compliance
3. PLACE and PACE (Playful, Loving, Accepting, Curious, Empathy and Playful, Accepting, Curious, Empathy)
4. Intersubjectivity
5. Reflective Capacity
6. Affective/Reflective dialogue
7. Commitment
8. Insightfulness

9. Coherent Narrative
10. Co-law of feelings
11. Co-advent of that means
12. Follow-lead-follow
13. Interactive repair
14. Nonverbal-verbal dialogue

A few of the fundamental concepts of Dyadic Developmental Psychotherapy can be summarized withinside the following 4 paragraphs.

1. Both the caregivers' and therapist's personal attachment techniques are prepared and resolved earlier than the onset of the kid's remedy. Previous research (Tyrell et al. 1999; Dozier et al. 2001) has proven the significance of the caregivers' and therapist's country of thoughts with recognize to attachment for right remedy outcomes.
2. The therapist and caregiver offer the intersubjective reviews for the kid that have been seldom found in conditions of abuse and neglect. These intersubjective reviews are characterised with the aid of using shared emotion (affect), attunement, shared attention and attention, and complementary intentions. Intersubjective reviews are the number one approach with the aid of using which the little one and younger toddler learns approximately self, other, and the world (Trevarthen 2001). Complex trauma will drastically disrupt the improvement of the ability of the kid to interact in concordant intersubjectivity (attunement, shared attention, and shared and complimentary intentions) and growth the threat that the kid may be not able to create a coherent that means for plenty events, especially disturbing ones. The therapist should offer concordant intersubjective reviews for the discern that assist create a stable base inside which the discern, toddler, and therapist can co-create new and greater healing meanings for reviews. Whenever possible, the kid's number one caregiver (biological, adoptive, or foster discern or number one caregiver in a residential setting) is an lively player withinside the consultation. The therapist should offer to the caregiver assist and steerage in speaking thoughts, feelings, and intentions to the kid in a healing and concordant high-quality intersubjective manner. The number one caregiver serves because the number one supply of protection, security, and luxury at the same time as the kid explores events, reviews, and feelings which can generate worry and shame. The caregiver's presence permits the therapist to facilitate the a success exploration and backbone of conduct troubles withinside the domestic with the aid of using modeling for the discern PACE (Playful,

Accepting, Curious, Empathic, defined greater completely below) as an powerful approach of reaching struggle decision and growing emotional and behavioral law in the domestic. The therapist will usually best see a toddler, commonly a teenager, as an person consumer whilst a number one attachment discern isn't available. In these

instances, the remedy will continue at a markedly slower tempo in view that the kid is basically emotionally by myself the relaxation of the week withinside the technique of integrating the healing themes. The loss of a number one attachment discern is a intense obstacle to developing the safety and protection important for exploration and integration.

3. Use of PACE and PLACE. These acronyms describe the "mindset" of the therapist and caregiver. PACE refers back to the therapist putting a restoration tempo of remedy via way of means of being playful, accepting, curious and empathic. Through PACE, the therapist is capable of each generate and alter, thru empathy (and playfulness whilst appropriate), the rising emotion this is related to the occasions being explored. Positive concordant intersubjective stories are in large part created with PACE. The therapist is likewise capable of facilitate an open, reflective mindset to reorganize the enjoy of those occasions thru the therapist's accepting and curious stance. PLACE refers back to the figure developing a restoration surroundings via way of means of being playful, loving, accepting, curious and empathic. All interventions are applied in the context of PACE/PLACE together with the opposite concepts provided on this monograph. Any method may also result in dysregulation if those fundamental concepts, which can be had to generate standard safety, are ignored. These thoughts are defined in extra element in Becker-Weidman, (2010), Becker-Weidman, (2011), Becker-Weidman and Shell (2011), Becker-Weidman and Shell (2010), and Hughes (2006, 2007, 2009).

4. The inevitable misattunements and conflicts that get up in relationships are at once addressed and repaired thru the continuing features of the connection the use of PACE for interactive restore. The advent of concordant intersubjectivity allows the co-advent of that means and the co-law of emotions. In different words, conducting a positive, emotionally significant courting with attunement, shared attention, and complimentary intentions allows the customer learn how to alter emotions. It is the sharing of this enjoy that allows have

an effect on law and the improvement of a coherent autobiographical narrative. The want for interactive restore is specifically crucial because the issues being explored are frequently characterised via way of means of disgrace and fear. Repair allows with each have an effect on and behavioral law. Repair at once addresses the kid's convictions, primarily based totally on beyond bad stories of forget and abuse, that the kid have to face stressful

occasions on my own or that any battle will result in abandonment. The attachment figures are liable for the initiation of restore, now no longer the kid. These equal concepts follow to the therapist-caregiver courting. Inevitable misattunements among therapist and figure are at once addressed and repaired thru the connection. It is the therapist's obligation to provoke the restore, now no longer the figure.

## THERAPIST USE OF SELF

A chippie makes use of levels, saws, nails, and hammers. The Dyadic Developmental Psychotherapist makes use of self. Use of self through the therapist is on the center of the way Dyadic Developmental Psychotherapy is implemented. Use of self entails the introduction and protection of concordant intersubjective studies: the sharing of one's studies of the alternative in a healing manner. This use of self is continually centered on assisting the patron obtain extra self-expertise, greater bendy modes of relating, and greater proper emotional studies that mirror the character and excellent of the present day relationship. All the alternative additives of Dyadic Developmental Psychotherapy are enacted thru the therapist's use of self. PACE is basically a characteristic of the therapist's use of self in a healing manner. The healing use of self calls for a well-advanced reflective characteristic and stable country of thoughts with recognize to attachment. As the therapist creates concordant intersubjective studies, the therapist video display units the impact on the alternative and the alternative's emotional revel in. The intention is to create emotionally significant studies that facilitate the combination of recollections and feelings that had been dissociated (cut up off) because the end result of early relational trauma. The therapist should continuously reveal the alternative's affective country to hold the interactions emotionally significant and now no longer dysregulating (Becker-Weidman, Ehrmann, LeBow, 2012). The therapist's use of self entails maintaining up an affective/reflective communicate amongst own circle of relatives members. By reflecting on and tracking the at once taking place studies, the therapist continues a stability among the affective and the reflective factors of the communicate. The healing use of self as defined right here is what lets in for the introduction of a brand new and coherent autobiographical narrative, the co- law of feelings, and the co-introduction of recent meanings. Much of this takes place on a non-verbal degree thru using tone of voice, volume, gestures, cadence, facial expressions, and modulation of voice: the verbal-

non-verbal communicate. In order to assist the patron discover doubtlessly painful and demanding recollections, feelings, and studies, the therapist consciously follows the patron (thru recognition and interest), then leads the patron deeper, and once more follows at this deeper degree. Finally, whilst inevitable misunderstandings arise, the therapist should be capable of manipulate the revel in of disgrace in order that the therapist can be given duty for the therapist's mistake. By acknowledging one's errors, mistakes, and misjudgments, the primary steps towards interactive restore can occur. In this manner, the therapist fashions with the caregiver how the caregiver can reply to the kid whilst there may be a breach in that relationship.

To efficaciously and therapeutically use self, the therapist should have a exceedingly stable country of thoughts with recognize to attachment, fairly advanced reflective abilities, exact self-awareness, and be tolerant of ambiguity. A stable country of thoughts with recognize to attachment has been determined to be critical in healing work (Tyrell, et. al., 1999). A stable country of thoughts with recognize to attachment lets in the therapist to revel in a number of feelings and to mirror on those feelings in a exceedingly independent manner. Self-expertise entails being privy to private biases and being capable of mirror on inner states. The therapist should be privy to how a good deal an revel in displays the present day interactions with the alternative and what kind of displays private beyond records being evoked through the present day interactions. Finally, tolerance for ambiguity is an critical detail to be used of self due to the fact this prevents the therapist from upfront leaping to conclusions concerning what the alternative is experiencing and the which means the alternative ascribes to the studies. This suspension of fact lets in the therapist to shape diverse hypotheses concerning the which means of studies even as maintaining an open thoughts, in order that the therapist's interest can emerge in an proper and emotionally significant manner. Uncertainty promotes interest and questions with an emotional tone that mirror real hobby in and recognition of the alternative's thoughts, feelings, meanings, and studies. Finally, ongoing session may be a great useful resource on this work. Consultation can guide the therapist in exploring the therapist's very own studies and use of self.

## IT'S ABOUT CONNECTIONS NOT COMPLIANCE

Relationships (friendly, intimate, or therapeutic) are constructed on connections or reports which have emotional that means and cost. The Dyadic Developmental Psychotherapy therapist focuses by and large on relationships and connections, now no longer compliance. It isn't that compliance isn't crucial; it is. However, the manner to stable authentic and genuine compliance is thru connections and relationships. This is an crucial idea for caregivers to combine into their parenting. It is thru connections that the kid will internalize the figure's "voice" and increase impulse control, morals, values, and extra effective social functioning. The tale of Pinocchio, in a few respects, illustrates this. As lengthy as Jiminy Cricket become on Pinocchio's shoulder, Pinocchio become nicely behaved. However, on every occasion Jiminy Cricket become away, that become while Pinocchio were given into trouble; he had now no longer internalized "compliance." At the stop of the tale, Pinocchio turns into a "actual" boy while he is going off to keep his father, Gippetto. In different words, Pinocchio turns into a actual boy while he cares approximately another.

## PACE AND PLACE

PACE is the mindset of the therapist. It is the therapist's obligation to hold a recuperation tempo of treatment. It is an acronym for being Playful, Accepting, Curious, and Empathic. PLACE is the mindset of the caregiver. It is the caregiver's obligation to hold a recuperation place. It is an acronym for being Playful, Loving, Accepting, Curious, and Empathic. It paperwork the middle of ways the therapist or figure starts offevolved to discover an occasion or issue. PACE is likewise the number one approach of initiating "interactive repair" (defined below) for the duration of the consultation. This is needed on every occasion the kid initiates a spoil withinside the dating or the spoil is created through a misattuned initiative or reaction through the therapist or figure.

An instance of such an interplay might also additionally illustrate this procedure extra clearly. Sarah, age nine, is available in together along with her foster mom, Mary. In a assembly with the therapist earlier than the joint consultation, Mary reviews that "out of the blue" Sarah attacked her withinside the dwelling room whilst they had been cleansing up. Mary is disenchanted and says, "I'm now no longer certain if I can hold a baby in my domestic like Sarah who's so randomly and unpredictably aggressive." The joint consultation starts offevolved with Sarah, Mary, and the therapist.

T: Hi, Sarah. How are you?

S: I become terrible (stated in a smooth voice with head down and eyes on her knees. Sarah might be feeling shame. Notice her use of words. She says "I become terrible," now no longer "I did some thing terrible." This is NOT your cue to provide Sarah the lecture "Now, you recognise, Sarah, YOU aren't BAD, simply once in a while you do terrible things." Instead, I receive Sarah's view and discover it with interest to apprehend what it approach to Sarah. I need to go into her revel in together along with her).

T: What happened?

S: Well, I hit and kicked Mom the day past evening.

T: Well, what happened? (Notice, I do now no longer ask "Why did you do that?" Probably Sarah does now no longer recognise why she did it. Together we can discover "why.")

S: We had been cleansing up the dwelling room, and I knew she become mad at me. (Looking at her foster mom via the hair masking her eyes.)

Note, due to the fact I even have already met with Mary with out Sarah at the start of the consultation, Mary does now no longer have to break Sarah to "correct" Sarah's model of the events; Mary has already given her model to me and has felt that I understood and typical her view and concerns.

T: What become she mad at you approximately?

S: I didn't end my dinner, and she or he hates it once I waste food.

T: Oh, in order that made you mad, and you then definately hit her? (I provide my information or speculation of what happened, a possible "why.")

S: No, I wasn't mad; I become concerned what she'd do to punish me.

T: Then what happened? (I receive her declaration and circulate to deepen and discover her revel in).

S: After we wiped clean up dinner, she advised me to return back into the dwelling room to assist her easy up.

T: Oh, in order that's while you bought mad at her?

Note: The therapist does now no longer should be right. Expressing a tentative opinion and looking to apprehend Sarah indicates that I am inquisitive about Sarah, cost her, and our dating.

## INTERSUBJECTIVITY

As formerly described, intersubjectivity is shared affect, goal, and attention. Intersubjectivity may be concordant, while all 3 factors are in accord, or it could be discordant. When an interchange appears to be going awry, it's far beneficial to take into account which detail of the intersubjective revel in is discordant. Often, it is going to be that the intentions are discordant. An instance might also additionally serve to demonstrate this. In this instance, the therapist is speakme with a unmarried parent, Steve, approximately his son, Eric, age thirteen. Steve seems to be as an alternative important and punitive, and the therapist desires to assist Steve cognizance on what's riding Eric's conduct in preference to on floor conduct. However, on this instance, the interchange does now no longer pass properly.

Steve: I simply were given Eric's five-week report, and it's far awful. He's failing math and technological know-how and is slightly passing his different subjects. I informed him if he doesn't do higher, he'd be grounded till he does. I am so mad at him.

Therapist: OK, so that you need him to get higher grades. Why did he accomplish that poorly? (Problem fixing in preference to searching deeper)

D: Because he doesn't examine and neglected lots of homework.

T: I see, so that you determine you may get him to examine greater and do his homework if he's grounded and has no TV or pc or games?

D: Exactly!

T: You've carried out this before, and it hasn't worked. Why do you watched it'll this time? (Problem fixing. The therapist is now starting to sense irritated with Steve now no longer getting what they've pointed out before)

D: What else ought to I do? (Steve begins offevolved to emerge as defensive; no surprise) T: I assume you need to recognize that the manner to get him to do properly is through having a higher dating with him. "It's approximately connections now no longer compliance," is what I say. (This trouble fixing intellectualized declaration has a sturdy undertone of blame. Perhaps the therapist is feeling that he has to guard Eric. This is in which the therapist should have moved the interchange right into a concordant intersubjective revel in.)

D: What, so I'm imagined to be his pal and forget about his horrific grades? (Now, Steve and the therapist are on contrary aspects of the fence and are arguing. They aren't engaged with every different in a concordant manner.)

T: No. What I suggest is the manner to get exact grades is to cognizance on having a dating with him in order that he desires to do properly. Right now he feels you're forcing him to do properly. (Here the therapist is starting to act as Eric's endorse, protecting him towards his father).

D: So what's incorrect with that?

T: What's incorrect with this is that now you're each in a manipulate struggle with Eric's grades. Privileges being the ammunition, you every are taking pictures at every different. (In addition, the therapist is in a manipulate struggle of kinds with the father).

It is going downhill from here. While what the therapist is announcing can be on target, the interchange isn't always concordant on the scale of goal or emotion. The therapist seems to be set on "explaining" what Steve ought to do, and Steve seems to be set on protecting his approach. They do now no longer have joint shared goal. It is likewise possibly that Steve can be feeling blamed through the therapist and that the therapist can be feeling irritated that Steve simply does now no longer "get it." Maybe the therapist is thinking, "Eric is a superb kid, if simplest Steve could see that." So the therapist starts offevolved to attempt to act as Eric's endorse and defender. This might also additionally then cause an interpersonal struggle among the therapist and Steve while the struggle among worrying approximately Eric and looking to have him get exact grades ought to be intrapersonal (inside Steve).

The following instance illustrates how focusing at the factors of intersubjectivity and what's discordant can cause a greater powerful interchange.

Steve: I simply were given Eric's five-week report, and it's far awful. He's failing math and ELA and is slightly passing his different subjects. I informed him if he doesn't do higher he'd be grounded till he does. I am so mad at him.

Therapist: You sound upset. (The therapist movements to
affect) D: You wager I am. I recognize he can do higher;
he's simply lazy!

(Now, the therapist may want to argue with Steve approximately whether or not or now no longer Eric is lazy or if he simply feels so awful approximately himself that he acts in a manner to verify his self-image, or perhaps that Eric's beyond studies have led him to experience not anything he does matters, so why try? However, as a substitute the therapist will live targeted on Steve for now to deepen their concordant intersubjectivity and hold all 3 dimensions in sync.)

T: You sound disillusioned or harm, perhaps that Eric isn't doing better.

D: I am disillusioned. I realize he can do better; he's a clever child. He may want to have a notable destiny if he carried out himself. (Steve is now speaking extra softly, and he seems extra somber).

T: You without a doubt love Eric and need him to do well, don't you?

D: Yes, I'm his Dad. I've been attempting for 4 years now, and I simply get so annoyed every so often that not anything I do makes a difference. What am I going to do?

T: Let's parent it together, OK? I'm positive we are able to give you something.

D: OK

T: You stated Eric is a vibrant child and will achieve this an awful lot better. What is your wager on why he doesn't? (The therapist has now created joint aim and attention: "we can parent this out together).

D: I simply assume he's lazy.

T: Education is without a doubt crucial to you, and you've stated that he may want to cross a long way together along with his brains, so what could make one of these child be lazy? (Here the therapist accepts Steve's view and attempts to head deeper via way of means of asking a question, via way of means of being curious.).

D: Maybe he in no way had every body train him the way to work?

T: You imply that perhaps, due to the fact he changed into so ignored as a younger child, he in no way discovered to position forth attempt and all the ones foster houses he changed into in in no way made him experience something mattered or that he mattered?

D: I in no way notion approximately it that manner, however yea, that makes sense, the terrible child. So what do I do now?

T: Well, let's parent out the way to assist him experience he's succesful and notice what you spot in him.

D: Well, punishing him like I've been doing doesn't work. All it possibly did, I now see, is verify that he's a failure and that I'm mad at him. How do I make that as much as him? (Because of the protection created via way of means of the therapist, Steve is capable of discover what he has been doing and remember alternatives.)

Within this concordant intersubjective enjoy, Steve and the therapist have performed  things. First, they have got deepened their relationship. The therapist knows Steve better, and Steve feels the therapist desires to assist him via way of means of know-how him. The therapist has modeled with Steve what the therapist might also additionally need Steve to do with Eric. Second, they co-created a brand new which means for Eric's terrible grades that results in a exclusive and extra powerful set of behaviors.

# REFLECTIVE CAPACITY

Reflective capability refers back to the capability to concurrently be in an enjoy and so that it will reflect onconsideration on that enjoy. Peter Fonogy (Fonogy, et. al. 2002) describes this as mentalizing. It approach having a intellectual

illustration of self, other, and the relationship. This intellectual illustration lets in one to expect the other's capability actions, feelings, and mind after which act accordingly. It is the premise for empathy, the capability to peer and experience with the other. Obviously, the therapist ought to have a well-evolved reflective feature. One of the desires of remedy is to decorate and broaden the caregiver's reflective capability and to broaden and decorate the child's reflective capability. The reflective feature is important for impulse control. It offers that 1/2 of a 2d of pause, to be able to remember a reaction in the context of what one believes the other's aim, feelings, and mind are.

A quick instance will serve to demonstrate the reflective feature. In this case that came about close to the give up of remedy, Aaron, age fourteen, is describing to me how his start mom harm him and his siblings.

Aaron: And then Emma (his stArt mother) could hit Lindsey and Bobby. She'd use the steel fry pan and it changed into horrible. Oh, Dr. Art, I'm now no longer converting the subject, I simply need you to realize how my mother harm me and my sister and brothers. OK?

In this example, Aaron describes what took place and it additionally exemplifies the operation of the reflective feature. In order for Aaron to make the closing statement, "Oh, Dr. Art, I'm now no longer converting the difficulty..." he needed to have a intellectual illustration of me, the discussion, and his intentions. While speaking, he found out that I may count on he became converting the difficulty through speaking approximately his siblings and now no longer himself. So, he tells me what his aim is and assures me he isn't always converting the difficulty. To do that Aaron needed to have a intellectual illustration of ways I assume and of our relationship.

# AFFECTIVE/REFLECTIVE DIALOGUE

An affective/reflective talk may be defined as a communication that consists of emotional, reflective, and cognitive elements. It is a comfortable and meandering talk that has a story-telling best to it. In many ways, the affective/reflective talk describes the ebb and go with the drift of a communication wherein there's an enjoy with emotional valance after which a few mirrored image approximately the enjoy. There is emotional engagement on this talk. This comfortable and meandering talk frequently side-steps resistance for the reason that patron is

an energetic player withinside the talk and the ensuing co-introduction of meaning.

# COMMITMENT

The therapist's dedication is to the own circle of relatives; to assist the own circle of relatives come to be a "happier" place. To reap this, the therapist can also additionally locate that the therapist's number one dedication will must be to the mother and father on account that they're the keystone for restoration and a a hit outcome.

Many therapists skilled as infant therapists locate themselves withinside the awkward function of feeling, "If simplest the mother and father might get a grip, this infant might be fine." What then frequently occurs is that the therapist starts to experience and act as the kid's advocate, talking for the kid and looking to persuade the mother and father to be higher mother and father. This direction regularly results in an deadlock or to the own circle of relatives discontinuing treatment.

If the mother and father have problems that impair their abilties to create a restoration place, the therapist use of PACE and the affective/reflective talk allows create a steady base on the way to permit the mother and father to discover what's interfering with their being the kind of mother and father they would really like to be. The therapist makes use of PACE to sign up for with, accept, apprehend, and aid the mother and father in order that the mother and father can accept, apprehend, and aid their infant. "Whatever the therapist needs the mother and father which will do with their infant, the therapist has which will do with the mother and father," (Becker-Weidman, 2010, 2011). This paperwork the bedrock of the therapist's stance regarding the number one caregivers.

# INSIGHTFULNESS

Insightfulness is associated with the reflective feature defined above. To be insightful approach to appearance inside, "in" "sight." Insight includes the cappotential to appearance inside and to greater deeply apprehend one's self, one's reasons and intentions, and the way those had been formed through beyond and modern stories, relationships, and events.

Insight lets in the therapist to higher apprehend what feelings are being activated through the therapist's beyond stories and which feelings are being activated through the modern stories. Developing insightfulness amongst own circle of relatives participants is one of the vital obligations of the therapist training Dyadic Developmental Psychotherapy.

The therapist accomplishes this the use of the affective/reflective talk, through

the co-introduction of meanings, through observe-lead-observe, through interactive restore, and through the verbal/non-verbal talk. The affective/reflective talk and the verbal/non-verbal talk are techniques through which perception is achieved. This talk with its emotional and reflective additives is how the patron achieves extra self-knowledge. When entered into, this talk is how new and greater useful meanings of stories are co-created. This talk is led through the therapist withinside the observe-lead-observe format.

Interactive restore guarantees that the inevitable errors that arise on this procedure are owned and general after which explored and repaired. It is in the protection of the steady base that the exploration vital to reap integration and restoration can arise. This integration and restoration takes place through exploring modern stories and their connections to beyond stories. By exploring how the beyond is alive withinside the present, the therapist assists the patron in accomplishing deeper insightfulness.

# COHERENT NARRATIVE AND THE CO-CREATION OF MEANING

The advent of a coherent autobiographical narrative is one marker of intellectual health. A private narrative adjustments over time, and it's miles this narrative that offers that means to one's lifestyles and reports. Those with stable styles of attachment are capin a position to inform coherent tales approximately their lives, no matter how hard the ones lives might also additionally were. A coherent autobiographical narrative displays the combination of the left mind hemisphere characteristic of containing specific reminiscences with proper hemisphere wherein have an effect on and implicit reminiscences are located. Trauma interferes with this integration. Without this integration, one's feel of self with a beyond, present, and destiny can come to be distorted, vague, and disconnected. Clients who've skilled complicated trauma often have disjointed, cut up-off, and dissociated autobiographical narratives. The episodic and emotional factors of the trauma are cut up off and disconnected from every other. While the emotional sequelae of the trauma are really glaring withinside the man or woman's behavior, the man or woman isn't aware about this. Revisiting the trauma in detail and in a titrated manner so that the emotions are experienced in the safe and secure setting of the therapy session and in the family allows for the integration of emotional and episodic memories and the conscious awareness of how these events and feelings are

running withinside the present. This insightfulness offers an crucial restoration measurement to remedy. Once dissociated factors are incorporated right into a coherent autobiographical narrative, the customer is capable of manipulate the underlying feelings and interact the reflective characteristic to choose the ideal and self-advancing response.

# CO-REGULATION OF EMOTIONS

Children and adults with hard histories frequently have now no longer obtained the essential reports that could permit them to successfully adjust their very own feelings. In maximum common circumstances, a determine first regulates the little one's emotional international and so regulates the little one's emotional reports. The "top enough" determine offers stimulation to set off the little one however is cautious now no longer to over-stimulate. The "top enough" determine (Winnicott, 1992, p. 17 and

p. 43) sooths the disillusioned little one and decreases distress. In this fashion, the determine regulates the little one and younger child's stage of arousal and emotional reports. Over time, the kid starts to internalize this shared co- law of have an effect on and turns into self-regulating. In this sequence, first the determine regulates the kid, then the kid is capable of obtain emotional law with the determine's help, after which the kid can self-adjust.

# FOLLOW-LEAD-FOLLOW

Follow-Lead-Follow describes the ebb and float of the talk in the Dyadic Developmental Psychotherapy consultation. This framework is designed to inspire customer engagement and to boom the customer's feel of safety, security, and private control. The therapist starts via way of means of the use of the PACE framework, accepting what the customer says. The therapist follows the customer's float of discussion and emotion and remains in line with the customer. The goal right here is to metaphorically stroll with and subsequent to the customer. This facilitates create a stable base via way of means of presenting the customer with recognition and a concordant intersubjective revel in. Client and therapist are sharing have an effect on and are getting to the identical thing. Intentions are conjoint and complimentary, so the therapist is interested by what the customer is interested by at that moment. The customer will sense valued due to the fact the therapist is that specialize in what the customer reveals of interest. Once the talk has moved alongside to a few degree, the therapist can then start to lead the customer right into a associated path

that has a exclusive trajectory. For instance, the therapist might also additionally start to notice how this case is much like one which happened withinside the beyond or touch upon what the customer might also additionally were feeling. The therapist leads the dialogue deeper. Once in this new trajectory, the therapist once more follows the customer and the cycle continues.

The therapist frequently takes the lead early in remedy to carefully offer the phrases for the kid, after which, if the phrases are recounted via way of means of the kid as correct representations of the kid's revel in and internal lifestyles, the therapist might also additionally "communicate for" the kid to the caregiver. The therapist might also additionally positioned into phrases what the therapist believes is the kid's revel in. The following instance illustrates those processes.

Parent: He had this type of suit the previous day after I introduced him to a brand new sitter for the day at the same time as I went to work

Therapist: Billy became without a doubt dissatisfied.

P: I don't realize why? He wouldn't inform me.

T: Billy, do you recognize what dissatisfied you the previous day?

Billy: (As he buries his head beneathneath the sofa pillow he mumbles in a pitiful voice) Sorry.

T: You sound dissatisfied Billy; can you are saying what dissatisfied you so? B: (he stays pretty and beneathneath the cushion).

T: Say, Billy, wouldn't it not be OK if I pretended to be you and communicate with a view to your mom?

B: (from beneathneath the cushion) yes.

T: If I get some thing wrong, will you allow me realize? B: OK

T: OK, I'm gonna communicate for Billy now. "Mom, I were given so scared while you introduced me to that area the previous day. I idea you have been going to depart me there and by no means come back."

The therapist's non-verbal expressions, tone of voice, and cadence are congruent with the phrases, and this could regularly permit the kid to revel in the speak with the determine as though the kid had absolutely stated the phrases to the determine.

# INTERACTIVE REPAIR

Interactive restore (Tronick 1989, Tronick 2005) describes how the therapist or determine responds to the inevitable breaches that arise in any dating all through the ebb and waft of revel in. Interactive restore refers back to the caregiver's (or therapist's) movements to restore the connection and to emotionally reconnect with and reestablish an attuned dating with the kid (or determine) after there was a breach withinside the dating. Interactive restore is the method with the aid of using which a caregiver maintenance a few misattunement withinside the dating in a way that reduces disgrace. Interactive restore ends in the improvement of extra ability to revel in terrible feelings with out resultant disgrace and dysregulation. Interactive restore calls for a caregiver who's touchy and collaborative. When the caregiver allows the kid get over a terrible affective state, the quantity of disgrace skilled is reduced. When the caregiver engages in interactive restore on a reasonably steady basis, the kid develops an inner revel in of self as effective, that the kid's intentions are nice, and that misery is reparable. These identical consequences of interactive restore practice whilst it's far the therapist who initiates interactive restore with a caregiver. This fashions for the caregiver the way to interact on this maximum important method.

The recuperation size of interactive restore is that it reduces disgrace. Interactive restore can assist a infant development developmentally from a disgrace- primarily based totally identification to the revel in of wholesome and suitable guilt. The determine putting a restriction may also reason the ruin withinside the dating, especially in a few detail of shared intersubjectivity, normally a discontinuity in shared emotion or joint complementary intention. A breach withinside the dating also can be due to an person false impression the kid or lacking crucial emotional cues. The disruption withinside the dating that takes place may also cause the kid experiencing disgrace. The cycle of experiencing nice have an effect on following terrible reports teaches the kid that terrible feelings may be tolerated and resolved and that the connection may be repaired. Over time because the wholesome determine reestablishes attunement, the kid starts offevolved to revel in the self as intrinsically good, even though as one that every so often does "awful" matters. It is that this motion from feeling that one is awful to feeling that one is right however does awful matters this is on the middle of the developmental step from disgrace to guilt.

Amos is ten years old. He became followed whilst he has six after a 3 year stint in six specific foster homes, a number of which have been almost as abusive as his start family. His adoptive father became abusive, and his adoptive mom (Erica) left the daddy whilst Amos became nine. Amos now lives together along with his adoptive mom and brother. In addition to Reactive Attachment Disorder and complicated trauma, Amos have been recognized with the aid of using a infant psychiatrist with Bipolar I Disorder and is on numerous specific psychotropic medications. Amos regularly pulls out his hair and choices at sores and his frame till he bled. The following interchange takes area in a 2d or 1/3 session, earlier than I knew Amos or his mom very well. We are all sitting on a sofa with Amos among me and his mom. This instance illustrates the therapist beginning interactive restore.

Therapist: That have to were so frightening for you whilst your start mother and father used to combat with every different like they did.

Amos: I guess (he is calling instantly ahead, with out an awful lot have an effect on present, except, as I cited in a while the tape of the session, his tapping foot).

Therapist: Your mother changed into telling me that your beginning dad and mom used to hit every different, and plenty of instances one or each were given genuinely hurt, and the police confirmed up.

A: Um.

Erica: Yes, that's what the social employees advised me. They stated whilst the police confirmed up Amos could be hiding below a mattress or in a closet

T: Oh, Amos, do you recall that? A:

Um.

T: You have to were so scared to listen and notice that. (I now be aware that Amos has picked his nostril and is wiping the blood on my left blouse sleeve.)

Note: Since it's far the therapist's activity to keep a restoration pace, I see what's going on as being as a result of my lacking cues that Amos changed into giving me in advance that he did now no longer need to speak approximately this topic. Since I did now no longer be aware the ones cues or respond, Amos has to elevate his voice, so that you could speak, for me to listen him. Once he changed into wiping blood on my blouse, I finally "heard" him.

T: (turning closer to Amos and catching his eye). Oh, Amos, I am so sorry, I didn't realise how frightening this have to be for you. I ought to have

observed sooner. Do you need to forestall speakme approximately this?

A: Yes!

T: OK, that's fine; do you believe you studied you may say that to me? Could

you are saying to me, "Dr. Art, I don't need to speak approximately my beginning mother anymore!"

A: OK, Dr. Art, I don't wanna speak approximately this anymore.

T: OK, let's speak approximately some thing else. What ought to we speak approximately?

## PRACTICE IN RESIDENTIAL TREATMENT SETTINGS

Dyadic Developmental Psychotherapy may be used efficiently inside residential remedy, organization home, and different congregate care settings. Clearly all of the factors mentioned on this monograph may be used with youngsters in foster care; the foster dad and mom are the number one caregivers. In residential remedy settings, the childcare team of workers characteristic both as co-dad and mom with the kid's dad and mom or because the number one caregivers. When training this method in residential remedy settings, the therapist will contain the care team of workers with the kid in remedy, to the quantity that that is possible. The extra carefully the care team of workers characteristic as number one caregivers, the extra efficiently can the underlying trauma and attachment disturbances be resolved. All of the additives and ideas of remedy defined on this monograph may be included into the milieu of the residential care facility. However, it's far vital to apprehend that a software the use of an attachment version of care operates in another way than one the use of a behavioral version of care. Specific schooling for the team of workers is essential to put into effect any such version of care. My experience training staff in residential program around the world is that with the proper training these staff can become a very powerful therapeutic influence in the child's life and the resulting change can be dramatic. The use of Dyadic Developmental Psychotherapy in residential settings is defined completely elsewhere (Blackwell & McGuill, 2011; Clark, 2011)

# THE LIMITS OF EXPERIENCE

In this segment, I would love to bear in mind the bounds of revel in. What is experience? How can we use experiences with a client and how can we remain mindful that experience is not fact but may contain various biases that affect what we experience? Consider the experience of meeting a new client for the first time, a figure. I greet the character and as I start to speak my revel in of "humans like this," turns into clearer and extra firmly rooted. I "know" that humans like this generally tend to act in a specific way; perhaps that is primarily based totally on my revel in with different dad and mom who fit positive factors of my cutting-edge or beyond revel in. How may my judgment of this figure have an effect on my medical conduct with this figure? The exercise of Dyadic Developmental Psychotherapy calls for a aware attention of the numerous biases and bounds of revel in. Experience is filtered via and changed via way of means of beyond reviews. We come to decisions, judgments, and opinions, typically with out an awful lot aware attention or deliberation. In this segment I would love us to bear in mind those biases and bounds of revel in in order that we may also use revel in in a taken into consideration and open manner, spotting limits, last open to new perspectives, new methods of experiencing, and new judgments.

The reliance on enjoy is an critical a part of many varieties of psychotherapy. Nevertheless, how dependable is enjoy? How correct is enjoy? When I country, "That's my enjoy," is that reality, opinion, reality, or a partial illustration of reality? This article describes the biases that could distort enjoy and the results of those biases for experientially primarily based totally medical exercise. As Kahneman (2011a) states, "Whether you country them or now no longer, you frequently have solutions to questions which you do now no longer absolutely understand, counting on proof you could neither give an explanation for nor defend," (Kahneman, 2011a, p.97).

Experience is the set of impressions, feelings, and tendencies in the out-of-consciousness thoughts that deliver upward push to beliefs, attitudes and intentions in our aware thoughts. Experience is essentially the aware enjoy of "I" or "me" and consists of beliefs, attitudes, and intentions. These beliefs, attitudes, and intentions, however, are grounded in and a mirrored image of the impressions, feelings, and tendencies of the out-of-consciousness thoughts.

Broadly speakme consciousness and enjoy are composed of minds. The aware thoughts is essentially enjoy as the "I" or "me." This aware thoughts is firmly grounded in and linked to the "out-of- consciousness" thoughts. When we recollect it, this out-of-consciousness-thoughts honestly is the bigger controller of what we think about as enjoy. So a whole lot of what's done, said, thought, or felt arises from the out of consciousness thoughts. We talk, act, and think, and this is essentially automatic, rising completely fashioned like Athena from the brow of Zeus.

One of the primary "not unusualplace factors" or elements in powerful remedy is "the courting."(Lambert, 2004) The therapist-patron courting and the parent-infant courting are vital recovery factors of remedy. Experience and the inter-subjective sharing of enjoy make a contribution drastically to suitable results in psychotherapy and in parenting (Becker-Weidman & Hughes, 2009). Some fashions of remedy depend extra substantially at the intersubjective sharing of enjoy as a center aspect of remedy, consisting of Dyadic Developmental Psychotherapy (Becker-Weidman, 2010), many interpersonal-therapies, attachment facilitating parenting (Becker-Weidman & Shell, 2010), attachment-targeted remedy (Becker-Weidman, Ehrmann, & Lebow, 2012), and psychodynamic procedures, amongst others. These procedures obtain their effects through operating in and thru the courting. It is thru the character and fine of the alliance advanced and nurtured that alternate occurs. These procedures area terrific emphasis on developing an alliance and preserving the alliance in order that exploration can occur, which ends up in integration and recovery (Becker- Weidman, 2010).

The exercise of experiential psychotherapies locations sure needs at the therapist that can be much less obvious than in different procedures. One of those needs is the popularity and acknowledgement of the bounds of enjoy. Experience is a effective alternate agent (Becker-Weidman, 2010). However, there are substantial barriers to the usage of enjoy in remedy. Often clinicians and others make the statement, "That is my enjoy," as though this is reality and reality and consequently now no longer open to debate, difference, or discussion. The phrase, "That is my enjoy," is that person's man or woman enjoy, however it isn't enjoy withinside the feel that it represents reality or goal reality. The biases and distortions created through the operation of thoughts are crucial barriers to be considered.

When we mirror at the kingdom of our thoughts, we come to realise that what we consider "me," or "I" is really best a tiny a part of our thoughts; it's far the aware thoughts. The bulk of our revel in takes place outdoor of cognizance. When we mirror on revel in, we realise that every phrase isn't parsed and every sentence isn't completely fashioned earlier than speaking; it's far one lightly flowing clean process. The equal takes place for beliefs, impressions, and intentions. This 2d a part of thoughts is what I time period the out-of-cognizance thoughts. An instance can also additionally illustrate this.

When requested what's six plus six, twelve right now jumps to thoughts with none idea or attempt. However, while requested what's 100 seventy plus 3 hundred and fifty nine, a solution does now no longer right away come to thoughts. It takes intellectual attempt and targeted interest to determine it out. The biases I could be discussing function withinside the out-of- cognizance thoughts and have an effect on the aware thoughts's beliefs, attitudes, and intentions. Another detail is that the aware thoughts is regularly lazy, counting on what the out-of-cognizance thoughts feeds to it. For instance, a person is informed that a pen and pencil set cost $2.20 and the pen charges one greenback extra than the pencil. The character is then requested, "What does the pencil cost?" What is the primary element that pops into thoughts? The out-of-cognizance thoughts produces a solution and the aware thoughts accepts it without considering its accuracy[1].

An instance from regular lifestyles can also additionally serve to demonstrate some factors of those biases and ensuing distortions that I could be discussing. The aware thoughts is regularly guided through emotion instead of through reason, may be effortlessly swayed through small details, and is ignorant of its biases. At a residential remedy center, one of the therapists desired to start the use of an attachment version of remedy. The proposed extrade did now no longer suit with the scientific director's in large part subconscious impressions, feelings, and dispositions, so her preliminary response become negative. These impressions, feelings, and dispositions brought about aware attitudes, beliefs, and intentions grounded withinside the out-of-recognition thoughts. The advent of an attachment version of remedy on a pilot foundation could have prolonged the middle's programming to a populace that changed into in large part doing poorly below the behavioral version of remedy. The blessings to the middle could be extra powerful remedy for this tough to deal with populace and a broader variety of application services. What biases may also had been working here? First, the thoughts creates constant and coherent narratives. The medical director changed into properly versed in cognitive behavioral remedy and changed into educated as a conduct therapist in her graduate internship. The medical director's "story" changed into that remedy interventions and the milieu of the remedy middle ought to consciousness at the behaviors of concern. Anything that counters that influence can be rejected (see cognitive dissonance and affirmation bias below). Second, the "new" concept inspires uncertainty and that feeling then ends in the influence that the concept itself ought to be poor (see selective interest and the phantasm of validity, defined below). The medical director changed into very snug the use of behavioral remedy procedures and changed into now no longer as acquainted with attachment fashions of remedy. This is an instance of the sensation using the analysis, of the out-of-recognition thoughts directing the aware thoughts. Third, selective interest and affirmation bias result in a discounting of proof to the contrary (additionally see "What you notice is all there is"). Fourth, an "have an effect on heuristic" is working here. In this example the colleague's thoughts substituted the solution to an smooth question (How do I experience approximately this concept?) for the more difficult question (What do I reflect onconsideration on it? What is the proof?). Fifth, reports that aren't congruent with one's real revel in are frequently discounted, ignored, or rejected. In this example, the medical director had no direct revel in the use of or supervising others the use of an attachment-version of remedy and felt uncomfortable with it. Therefore, the medical director rejected the method and fashioned a notion and end constant with that feeling; she created a constant coherent story. The reality that the therapist stated correct effects with the brand new method in a preceding putting did now no longer matter. Nor did the numerous articles and studies research furnished to the medical director appear to make a whole lot of a distinction withinside the medical director's opinion. The medical director exempted herself "from the conclusions of experiments that surprised" her (Nisbett and Borgida,

1975). Her "intuitions will supply predictions which are too excessive and he or she have a tendency to position an excessive amount of religion in them," (Kahneman, p. 194). Sixth, the convenience of retrieval of assisting fabric for the sensation will upload self belief to the influence, a good way to lead the aware thoughts to experience self belief and actuality withinside the notion generated. The out-of-recognition thoughts is an associative thoughts; it collects and connects impressions, feelings, and reminiscences linked with and constant with the instantaneously matter. The out-of-recognition thoughts does now no longer don't forget or shape institutions with what can be missing. This is an example of, "What you notice is all there is." In this example, due to the fact the medical director feels poor approximately the proposed pilot application, motives for negating the concept spring without problems to thoughts and similarly help the medical director's notion. Remember, the aware thoughts works at the statistics this is retrieved from memory, in an automated and involuntary manner, that's the operation of the out-of-recognition thoughts. This is an instance of the "What You See Is All There Is" bias this is defined below. These biases in revel in then result in a fixed of attitudes, beliefs, and intentions grounded withinside the out-of-recognition thoughts which are skilled withinside the aware thoughts. The aware attitudes, beliefs, and intentions aren't examined. The supply of bias isn't always considered, and the issues in common sense aren't considered. Considering the biases takes intellectual attempt and the directing and focusing of interest, that's what the aware thoughts does. However, withinside the absence of compelling motivation to do so, the aware thoughts, the "I," normally is predicated at the impressions, feelings, and tendencies of the out-of-recognition thoughts.

This phase will describe a number of those essential boundaries to enjoy in order that clinicians higher recognize a way to use and interpret enjoy and in order that the clinician can higher replicate on how the enjoy of someone, event, and courting may be distorted with the aid of using those boundaries. The purpose isn't always to denigrate enjoy. The intuitions of an professional, grounded in substantial stories, may be powerful. The clinician who's capable of make an correct analysis quickly, the clinical practitioner who diagnoses a complicated contamination at a glance, the professional who can length up a scenario and are available to an correct judgment in an immediate are all examples of the strength of professional intuition. The undertaking is that an professional's self belief in judgment, intuition, and enjoy can be the identical stage of self belief a non-professional will enjoy concerning intuitions, judgments, and stories, distorted with the aid of using the biases defined on this phase. The purpose of this phase is to problematic at the limits of enjoy so that you can higher recognize our personal perceptions and stories and people of the individuals who come to us for assist in order that we aren't misguided. These boundaries constitute biases that have an effect on perceptions and the way and what we enjoy. Intuitions are guided with the aid of using numerous heuristics, or "policies of thumb," and those heuristics can lead us off track at times. The out-of-cognizance thoughts (subconscious thoughts) produces impressions, feelings, and tendencies mechanically grounded in associative memory. These subconscious thoughts operations are then typical with the aid of using the aware thoughts and come to be attitudes, beliefs, and intentions, except we exert attempt to direct interest and intellectual attempt withinside the use of govt features to assess those impressions, feelings, and tendencies. The article will give up with some recommendations for countering those subconscious biases and distortions of enjoy.

In this newsletter I will talk numerous limits to enjoy:

1. Selective Attention
2. Confirmation Bias & Cognitive Dissonance
3. The phantasm of validity
4. What you spot is all there may be & the tendency to create coherent stories
5. The fallacy of self belief v proper intuitive expertise

## Selective Attention

Selective interest limits our enjoy with the aid of using proscribing what we will attend to in any moment. Since interest is a chief detail of enjoy and one of the 3 number one additives of the intersubjective[2] sharing of enjoy, boundaries in our ability to attend, selective attention, will at once have an effect on and bias enjoy. Understanding this trouble permits us to be extra open and accepting of differing stories of the "identical" event.

We all have selective interest, getting to that that's maximum salient. Most often, what we attend to isn't always pushed with the aid of using aware intent, but

is a characteristic of our beyond stories, present day emotional and mental states, and what have an effect on from the beyond can be brought on with the aid of using components of the gift. All this happens out of doors of cognizance and mechanically with the aid of using components of our thoughts that aren't grounded in our aware govt features. We understand that humans who've skilled trauma may also show "supply attribution errors." (Briere & Lanktree, 2011). Affect or implicit recollections can be evoked with out the related episodic or specific factors being gift. The character then attributes the have an effect on from the beyond this is being brought on withinside the gift to a few character or scenario withinside the gift: supply attribution error. This could be one detail of selective interest. If beyond stories have sensitized someone to sure expectations, then the character will attend to the ones factors extra closely. Since there may be a restricted ability to take care of all of the stimuli available, the customer will attend to what's maximum salient: that is selective interest.

Therapists and others aren't proof against this phenomenon, so our revel in withinside the second might be biased via way of means of our selective interest, via way of means of our getting to a few factors of the revel in to the exclusion of others. A first rate video that truely illustrates that is the "Selective Attention" video on YouTube (Simmons & Chabris, 1999) and is defined withinside the ee-e book via way of means of those identical authors, The Invisible Gorilla (2011). In this video, a gorilla crosses the degree at the same time as the viewer has been advised to rely the range of time the gamers on one group byskip a ball to every different. Because of selective interest, simplest approximately one-1/2 of of the visitors see the gorilla. Yet they may be pretty assured that there has been no gorilla, till the tape is rewound. We need to understand that the statement, "That's my revel in," at the same time as reflecting the person's certainty, is the person's revel in filtered via selective interest of a circumspect variety of attended to factors withinside the modern-day scenario. This isn't always similar to truth or truth. As professionals, we need to be privy to this technique and continue to be open to the opportunity that our revel in is incomplete or maybe improper due to selective interest.

## Confirmation Bias & Cognitive Dissonance

Confirmation bias (Risen & Gilovich, 2007) refers back to the tendency of human beings to don't forget events, records, and reports that verify pre-current biases and to bargain or maybe overlook events, records, and reports that aren't congruent with the ones ideals. Because the out-of-focus thoughts is an associative thoughts, it simplest connects with and pals factors that verify. It is associated with the halo impact, wherein in advance reports and primary impressions strongly shadeation later impressions and ideals, probably main to sizeable bias in later revel in.

Confirmation bias ends in an automated choice for records and arguments which might be regular with modern-day ideals.

Cognitive dissonance (Festinger, 1957) is comparable in lots of respects to affirmation bias. Cognitive dissonance refers back to the tendency of human beings to bargain reports, events, and records that don't comply with ones ideals or biases and to search for and locate fabric that conforms to their ideals and biases. Again, the out-of-focus thoughts is associative and so it pulls recollections regular with one's feelings, ideals, and impressions. The out- of-focus associative thoughts does now no longer look for recollections or records that disconfirm its preliminary impressions.

These cognitive techniques are grounded withinside the automated structures of the thoughts, carefully associated with what Bowlby (1988) called inner running fashions. Experience is filtered via those lenses. If the modern-day scenario may be very just like the beyond wherein the ones inner running fashions developed, then those biases may also have a minimum bias impact on modern-day revel in. However, the biases nevertheless exist, and clinicians want to be privy to those biases in order that the aware factors of thoughts and the government features can examine those automated impressions and ideals.

The automated factors of thoughts soar to conclusions that the aware thoughts commonly accepts due to the fact those conclusions and ideals experience proper and true. The automated factors of thoughts perform in an associative manner, connecting various factors which have a few connection after which making different connections. However it simplest considers what's gift and perceived (What you spot is all there is). Only the aware thoughts can recall what can be lacking or what different objects or records want to be taken into consideration to assess the validity of the notion and conclusion.

For example, recall the sentence, "It changed into 2:30 withinside the afternoon as John rushed towards the financial institution; he stumbled and fell." The photo that possibly got here to thoughts changed into of a person jogging alongside a sidewalk, tripping, and falling as he changed into going towards a financial institution building. There possibly changed into no different opportunity photo or thought. However, recall that there are, in truth, different opportunities for this ambiguous sentence. John may also have simply gotten out of a ship and stumbled as he changed into hurrying up the financial institution of the river.

## What You See is all There is

"What you notice is all there may be" (Kahneman, 2011a) and what you notice and revel in is a constrained slice of what there may be. We ought to keep in mind that due to the fact human beings are super storytellers, we create coherent narratives primarily based totally on little facts. We will fill withinside the blanks and create a coherence this is frequently now no longer present. We make up memories primarily based totally on little facts after which act on our memories as though those structures are entire and real, regardless of the reality that what we see is all there may be and the inferences which might be the narrative we create are grounded in our very own biases and beyond revel in.

This chronic advent of a coherent narrative is grounded in numerous biases. One, of course, is our beyond revel in and the way that results in selective attention. The moves of affirmation bias and cognitive dissonance are different elements. A 1/3 ability bias is our tendency to expect consistency. Our reminiscence routinely and constantly updates this narrative approximately our revel in, and this seeming coherence can result in over self assurance withinside the tale created, main to a discounting of alternatives (due to the movement of cognitive dissonance, amongst different heuristics). The self assurance we revel in is a sense of kinds and is normally now no longer grounded in a deliberative or maybe rational assessment of whether or not or now no longer the tale is accurate. Therefore, the prejudice in the direction of coherence withinside the narrative we create can result in over self assurance and the discounting of opportunity memories or narratives.

We create narratives to "explain" the facts. Consider the following facts: distinctly sensible guys usually marry much less sensible ladies. Why is that? We can likely give you a lot of psychological, Social, and different motives or memories. Now, remember the assertion that there may be a vulnerable correlation among the IQ's of spouses. What memories do you currently give you? If that is real, that the correlation among the intelligence of spouses much less is than 100% (much less than perfect), and that guys and ladies, on common, have comparable IQ scores, then it's far inevitable that on common distinctly sensible guys will marry much less sensible ladies and on common distinctly sensible ladies will marry much less sensible guys; that is the idea of regression to the mean. So, there may be no underlying tale; it's far simply a statistical artifact. The greater coherent the narrative, the greater self assurance we sense; that is the phantasm of validity. Impressions trump preferred information or reasoned thinking.

## The Illusion of Validity

When we sense a sure way, we have a tendency to hold that notion even withinside the face of records and occasions that have to lead us to sense otherwise. Daniel Kahneman (2011) calls this "the phantasm of validity," that's the cognitive equal of our seeing a visible phantasm that we keep to peer regardless of understanding that what we see is an phantasm. Our pre-conceptions approximately others, coupled with affirmation bias and cognitive dissonance, can lead us to disregard compelling proof that our perceptions are clearly incorrect. The actuality of our revel in can result in the phantasm of validity and to now no longer query our revel in and to now no longer remember alternatives, even withinside the face of compelling and competing revel in.

## The fallacy of Confidence vs. True Intuitive Expertise

I will cease this text through in brief discussing the difference among the fallacy of self assurance, or the phantasm of validity, and real intuitive expertise. The expert's instinct is clearly grounded in repeated and certain preceding revel in, difficult paintings to accumulate a basis of information and

institutions. This deep basis of revel in and know-how is then accessed with the aid of using the extremely good strength of the mind to make institutions. As Thomas Alva Edison stated, "Genius is 1% concept and 99% perspiration." It is the lengthy and repeated have a take a observe and revel in of the professional that builds the know-how base vital to study a scenario and make the institutions vital to attract a accurate conclusion, to intuit the fine diagnosis, response, or narrative. The professional is capable of generalize primarily based totally on a majority of these stories, furnished the professional's beyond stories were cautiously considered, mistakes stated and corrected, and options explored; it calls for regular comments on mistakes of judgment. In order to have faith in an intuitive judgment, matters should occur. First, the modern-day scenario should be sufficiently acquainted and ordinary to permit for predictions from modern-day cues. In different phrases, if the scenario is new and unfamiliar, then the intuitive judgments that increase from our associative thoughts could be much less reliable. The associative thoughts is right at generating coherent stories, however it'll produce coherence even if there's none. Second, there should be enough possibilities to analyze the clues and cues and for comments on mistakes in order that we are able to accurate our preliminary faulty judgments or impressions. In different phrases, we require possibilities to mirror on mistakes of judgment and analyze the character of these mistakes, what clues and cues have been neglected or mis-interpreted.

## Conclusions

What are we as clinicians to do withinside the face of those diverse biases? While being privy to those biases is a beginning, it's far inadequate. It is inadequate due to the fact our biases closer to consistency works towards having doubts approximately felt certainty. The impressions, tendencies, and emotions shaped with the aid of using our out-of-attention thoughts that jump into attention, (and that end up our revel in, as ideals, attitudes, and intentions) experience actual and proper and this ends in a sense of certainty. Using our aware thoughts to impeach our ideals and assumptions is a disturbing task. It takes the expenditure of intellectual strength with the aid of using focusing and directing interest and intellectual attempt to the

responsibilities of mirrored image and self-monitoring, amongst different executive
functions. Since maximum of the time the emotions, tendencies, and impressions that cause aware ideals, attitudes, and intentions are accurate enough, we don't normally direct our aware thoughts to impeach our assumptions, emotions, impressions, tendencies and ensuing ideals, attitudes, or intentions.

Maintaining an open thoughts is simpler stated than done. However, the quantity to which the clinician is cushty with now no longer knowing, with preserving or even growing ambiguity, is the quantity to which the clinician can start to mitigate a number of those biases in revel in. One manner to do that is to constantly take into account opportunity reasons and views. Recognizing that phrases may have exceptional meanings and spending time exploring that and thinking about which can assist us preserve open minds to options. Making a recreation of that is one manner to perform this. When I say, "I should move downtown to press a suit," it makes a distinction whether or not I am a tailor or an attorney. When I say aloud, "I noticed my aunt," you may ask me, "what color, is she? Is she a purple ant or a black ant?" Word video games are a first rate manner of growing this openness to opportunity meanings, that could remind one to assess and rethink one's revel in, to now no longer take it because the best fact.

Another manner is to take into account the alternative man or woman's revel in and perceptions. Empathy and attunement facilitate this. Being curious and asking questions simply to apprehend a person else due to the fact that man or woman is exciting are different ways (Becker-Weidman, 2010). When we preserve in our cognizance that what we suggest with the aid of using a word won't be the equal element as another, due to the fact the word itself is vague, then we may additionally end up greater touchy to thinking about options to, "Well, that is my revel in," stated as though this makes it fact and fact. It is a good deal simpler to observe the biases of revel in in others than in oneself. However, as we take into account those biases and the way they have an effect on another's revel in, we turns into higher capable of do the equal with our very own revel in.

Developing mindfulness is any other manner to keep away from a number of the biases to wondering and enjoy defined on this article. By growing and increasing our ability to dispassionately look at our personal

enjoy and thoughts, we're greater open to watching our enjoy and what our out-of-
focus thoughts is telling us (the aware thoughts). (Note: we generally tend to enjoy our aware thoughts as "I," but maximum of our thoughts, beliefs, and intentions arrive from our out-of-focus thoughts.)

Regular session with a relied on colleague is any other manner to notice and accurate biases and distortions that impact enjoy. Since it's miles plenty less complicated to find out those biases in others, the representative is in a higher function to assist the clinician do not forget how those biases are affecting the clinician's enjoy. It may be hard for the clinician to stay open to the observations of clinician bias and distortion in clinician enjoy. When the colleague is "merely" a colleague and now no longer a supervisor, it may be even less complicated for the clinician to push aside the observations of the colleague. Finally, over the years the representative and clinician can end up so entwined of their courting that they arrive to proportion comparable biases and distortions in enjoy. For that reason, it can be of price to extrade experts or use one of a kind experts in a few alternating manner.

Recognizing biases and distortions in enjoy and the way the out- of-focus thoughts influences the aware thoughts is a essential talent for clinicians who use experientially primarily based totally remedy methods. While this takes directed intellectual attempt and targeted awareness and attention (now no longer some thing the aware thoughts does easily), the consequences of this could be a greater beneficial healing enjoy. In addition, those capabilities may have sizable useful consequences on different relationships, each expert and personal.

Printed in Great Britain
by Amazon

39174491R10037